Seasoned
with Love

A Collection of Recipes from

Presbyterian Women
of

Foothi̇ Foothill Presbyterian Church *urch*
1162 W Merrill Ave
Porterville, CA 93257
559-782-0130

Printed in the U.S.A. by

Cookbooks by Morris Press
P.O. Box 2110 • Kearney, NE 68848

For information on having your cookbook printed, write for
our FREE information packet or call Toll-Free at 1-800-445-6621.

23304-I   1

Dedication

Reverend Luke and Eleanor Fritz

This recipe book is dedicated to the memory of Reverend Luke Fritz and in appreciation of his wife, Eleanor Fritz, who now lives in Corvalis, Oregon.

Luke was pastor of this church with Eleanor at his side for 27 years. He was a man who believed in the value and importance of ministering to young people. He not only helped create the ministry of Calvin Crest, he worked with other youth organizations such as Boy Scouts and Girl Scouts. He also worked as a youth pastor and was a school board member. He was a man of integrity and vision.

The story of the part Luke Fritz played in creating Calvin Crest will be found on the following page.

The History of Calvin Crest

Let me give you the history of how the property came to be Calvin Crest. When we moved from Arizona to California in 1952 we learned Presbytery was renting the "Y" camp at Lake Sequoia for two weeks each summer for its camping program — one week for senior high and one for junior high camp.

When Presbytery started talking summer camping again, Luke asked [why] Presbytery didn't own their own grounds. They said they had been looking for something but hadn't found anything. Luke responded, "Sounds to me like you haven't looked very hard!" They threw the "ball" back at him by naming him chairman of the committee to find a property!

The next summer, instead of taking our usual leisurely family camping vacation, we took numerous short trips to look at property for sale in the Sierra. On the last Sunday of our vacation, we decided to spend the day in Yosemite and attend church at the chapel there. On the way in [to Yosemite], we stopped at the ranger station to ask about properties that might be available in the area. The ranger, fairly new to the area, didn't know of anything but he said he would try to find out and for us to stop again on our way home. He still hadn't come up with anything at that time. As Luke was leaving the station, he walked by a short, white-haired gentleman on his way in. As Luke was about to get in the car, the ranger stepped to his doorway and called Luke back, introducing him to Dr. Wells. When Luke told him what he was looking for and what it was to be used for, Dr. Wells lamented that his property had been for sale but a gun club from Southern California had taken an option on it, hoping to buy it in a few months. He did, however, know of two other properties for sale in the area. Luke made a date to come

back in a couple of days to see them. When we drove into Dr. Wells' ranch, we said to each other, "Wouldn't this have been an ideal spot." We went with Dr. Wells to look at the other properties which still didn't seem right, so since our vacation was ending, property search was put on hold for that summer.

Several months later we received a call from Dr. Wells asking if we had located anything and, if not, would Presbytery be interested in his ranch? The gun club's option had run out but they didn't have the funds to buy it yet and wanted him to renew the option for another six months. Dr. Wells said he would rather sell it to Presbytery if they were interested. Luke immediately contacted the rest of his committee. That Saturday they all went to the Wells' Ranch and agreeing that was it, took a six-month "option to buy" on it and presented it to Presbytery.

Some members felt it was too expensive and too big and voted it down. But Luke was stubborn and kept bringing it up for vote at future Presbytery meetings until finally it was accepted. Those who opposed buying the property gave it its first name, Fritz's Folly. Asking price was $86,000 to be paid over ten years. About a year after the property was acquired, $60,000 worth of timber was sold off the property.

Luke became President of the first board of Calvin Crest and served on the board all the allowable time we were there — three years on and one year off. Luke's brother, Carl, referred to Calvin Crest as Luke's baby, and [Luke] carried that protective feeling to his death.

By Eleanor Fritz
From the Calvin Crest Cone, Autumn, 1996

Acknowledgments

We gratefully thank the Presbyterian Women's group and their many friends that furnished the wonderful recipes for this cookbook.

A big "Thank You" to the Cookbook Committee that gave many hours over a long period of time to put this book together for printing.

Committee Members
Carolyn Walter and Joan Pharis, Co-Chairpersons
Sue Fiske
Joy Harvey
Beverly Gustafson

A special thanks to our former church secretary, Joyce O'Neal for her help in organizing our beginning efforts.

And real appreciation goes to our church secretary, Nancy Williams, for the maximum effort in doing all the typing and final organization of the recipes.

Camperships Seasoned with Love

The proceeds from the sale of this cookbook will become a Calvin Crest Scholarship Fund for the members and friends of Foothill Community Presbyterian Church.

The fund will be used to help children and adults with scholarships that will help them to pay for camperships or retreat fees for time at Calvin Crest that might not otherwise be available to them.

From the Recipe Files of the Foothill Community Presbyterian Women

Appetizers
&
Beverages

Helpful Hints

• You won't need sugar with your tea if you drink jasmine tea or the lighter-bodied varieties, like Formosa Oolong, which have their own natural sweetness. They are fine for sugarless iced tea, too.

• Calorie-free club soda adds sparkle to iced fruit juices, makes them go farther, and reduces calories per portion.

• A different flavoring for tea: Instead of sugar, dissolve old-fashioned lemon drops or hard mint candy in your tea. They melt quickly and keep the tea clean and brisk!

• Most diets call for 8 ounces of milk and 4 ounces of fruit juice. Check your glassware. Having the exact size glass insures the correct serving amount.

• Make your own spiced tea or cider! Place orange peels, whole cloves, and cinnamon sticks in a 6 inch square cheesecloth. Bring up corners and tie with string. Add to hot cider or tea for 10 minutes (longer if you want a stronger flavor).

• Seeds and nuts, both shelled and unshelled, keep best and longest when stored in the freezer. Nuts in the shell crack more easily when frozen. Nuts and seeds can be used directly from the freezer.

• Always chill juices or sodas before adding to beverage recipes.

• When possible, float an ice ring in punch rather than ice cubes. This not only is more decorative, but also inhibits melting and diluting.

• Try placing fresh or dried mint in the bottom of hot chocolate for a zesty taste.

• One lemon yields about 1/4 cup juice; one orange yields about 1/3 cup juice. This is helpful in making fresh orange juice or lemonade!

• Never boil coffee; it brings out the acid and causes a bitter taste. Store coffee in the refrigerator or freezer to retain the fresh flavor.

• Always use COLD water for electric drip coffee makers. Use 1 to 2 tablespoons ground coffee for every cup of water.

• Cheeses should be served at room temperature (approximately 70°).

• When serving hors d'oeuvres on a silver tray, you may wish to protect it from acids by covering it with a layer of leafy green lettuce.

APPETIZERS & BEVERAGES

BEAN DIP

1 med. can spicy refried beans
1 pt. sour cream
1 pkg. taco seasoning
Grated cheese

Chopped tomatoes
Chopped green onions
Sliced green olives

First layer beans in serving dish. Add taco seasoning to sour cream and layer on top of beans. Next layer cheese, tomatoes, olives and green onions. Ready to serve.

Emma Geren

BUFFALO WINGS
(Hidden Valley Ranch)

24 chicken wings, drumettes
1/2 c. melted butter
1/4 c. hot pepper sauce (or less)

3 T. vinegar
1 pkg. Hidden Valley mix
1/2 tsp. paprika

Dip chicken in mixture of butter, pepper sauce, vinegar. Put in baking pan and sprinkle with dressing mix. Bake at 350° for 25 to 30 minutes. Sprinkle with paprika.

Beverly Gustafson

CHRISTMAS CHEESE BALL

16 oz. cream cheese, softened
4 oz. blue cheese, crumbled
2 T. bell pepper, finely chopped

2 T. pimiento, finely chopped
1 T. garlic salt

Dry pimiento by pressing in paper towel. Combine pimiento with all the ingredients until thoroughly mixed. Shape into ball shape in bowl. Let "age" overnight to combine flavors. These go well with Triscuits and is a family favorite any time of year. I frequently double the recipe.

Cindi Rogers

CHUTNEY-CHEESE APPETIZER

2 tsp. butter
1/4 c. slivered almonds
1 (8-oz.) pkg. cream cheese

1 sm. jar chutney
1/2 c. mayonnaise

Brown almonds in butter, stirring. With wire whisk blend mayonnaise and cheese. Spread on assorted crackers or on celery. One cup mixture makes 3 dozen appetizers.

Mildred Walters

FRANK NIPS

Cut skinless franks diagonally into 10 slices each. Sauté in butter. Marinate in French dressing with a drop of hot pepper sauce added. Serve on picks stuck in melon or whatever you desire. Make fancy by using cocktail onion between 2 franks.

Mildred Walters

GREEK APPETIZER DIP

1 jar julienne (California brand)
sun-dried tomatoes*
12 oz. Athenos brand feta cheese
(1½ blocks)*
1 sm. bunch FRESH basil, chopped
(save a couple sprigs for garnish)

3 cloves garlic, pressed
½ tsp. black freshly ground pepper
⅓ c. olive oil

Drain oil off tomatoes into large frying pan. Add olive oil. Chop tomato strips on a cutting board until they are chunks (not long and stringy). Put a spoon in the dish. Add tomatoes, garlic, pepper to oil and turn heat to medium and stir constantly. When it bubbles, add the chopped basil and stir until it is wilted. Set off burner. Chop the blocks of feta cheese in fairly small pieces (I make tiny cubes out of it). Stir cheese into the tomato mixture, then spread out on a large flat dish. (I use a Corning Ware with 1-inch sides.) Sprinkle on basil and decorate with a couple of sprigs of basil. Serve with low-fat crackers or Sunshine nonfat crackers. * These can be found in Save Mart.

Carolyn Walter

HOT ARTICHOKE-CHEESE DIP

8 oz. Jack cheese, grated
8 oz. cheddar cheese, grated
2 cans artichoke hearts, drained &
chopped (use artichokes in
WATER, not marinade)

1 sm. can green chilies, diced
½ c. mayonnaise

Put all into shallow casserole and bake at 350° for 20 minutes or until cheeses are thoroughly melted.

Mildred Walters

LAYERED CRAB TACO DIP

2 cans crab meat, drained
2 green onions, minced
½ c. diced cucumber
½ c. diced red onion
1 med. tomato, finely chopped
2 T. minced fresh parsley
¼ c. lime juice
¼ c. lemon juice

¼ c. orange juice
Salt & freshly ground pepper
2 (8-oz.) pkgs. cream cheese,
softened
¼ c. mayonnaise
1 avocado, peeled, seeded & diced
Tortilla chips to serve

Combine crab, green onion, cucumber, red onion, tomato and parsley. Combine juices in a small bowl. Stir in crab mixture. Salt and pepper to taste. Cover and

(continued)

2

refrigerate overnight. Combine cheese and mayonnaise. Spread over bottom of a serving platter. Spread avocado over cheese. Drain crab mixture, pressing out moisture. Spread mixture over avocado. Serve with tortilla chips.

Joan Pharis

SAUSAGE BALLS

3 c. Bisquick
1 lb. hot sausage, uncooked

1 lb. cheddar cheese, shredded

Combine Bisquick, crumbled sausage and cheese in large bowl. Mix well with spoon or pastry blender or hands. Roll into 1-inch balls. Bake at 350° for 15 to 20 minutes, until light brown.

Joan Pharis

SHRIMP DIP

1 can mushroom soup
1 (8 oz.) cream cheese, softened
1 can baby shrimp, cleaned

4 green onions, chopped
4 ribs celery, chopped
Curry powder to taste

Mix together and let set several hours to blend flavor before serving.

Beverly Gustafson

TACO COMPUESTA DIP

1 sm. can spicy refried beans
1 can jalapeño bean dip
1 c. sour cream
1 pkg. taco dip mix
2 lg. mashed avocados

Shredded Jack & cheddar cheese
Chopped tomatoes
Chopped olives
Chopped onions

Mix refried beans and bean dip and spread in a dish. Mix sour cream and taco dip mix and spread on top of bean mixture. Layer the remaining ingredients on top of mixture. Serve with tortilla chips. This dip can be made the day before and refrigerated until serving.

Kathie Gifford

TASTY NIBBLES

Mix well in a pan:

1 bottle Orville Redenbacher's
   popcorn oil
1 tsp. lemon pepper

½ tsp. garlic powder
1 tsp. dill weed
2 pkgs. Hidden Valley dry dressing

In a **large** container put 2 boxes oyster crackers. Pour pan contents over crackers. Stir frequently until all moisture is absorbed by crackers and none is left in bottom of container.

Emma Geren

GRANDFATHER'S LEMONADE

Boil equal amounts of white sugar and water for 10 minutes. Pour into sterilized jar; cover and chill. Use for lemonade.

Lemonade:

1 c. + 2 T. lemon juice, freshly
  squeezed
1 tsp. finely grated lemon rind

1 c. sugar syrup (recipe above)
3½ c. water

Taste and add a little more syrup if sweeter drink is desired. Pour over crushed ice in a tall glass. Garnish with slice of lemon over edge of glass and a maraschino cherry in the bottom. Made in 1895 for ladies' afternoon parties.

Carolyn Walter

EARTH SHAKES

2 bananas, peeled & frozen
2 c. apple juice

1 c. vanilla nonfat yogurt

Put bananas, then juice and then yogurt into a blender. Mix until smooth. Drink right away. This is a good drink for breakfast!

Cindi Rogers

PARTY PUNCH

5 lg. bottles 7-Up, chilled
½ gal. sherbet (orange, lime, berry,
  etc. - you may want to follow your
  color scheme)

Put this together just before serving. Mix a little, leaving small lumps floating. If making strawberry, you may want to float fresh strawberries.

Betty Baird

23304-98

Breads
&
Rolls

Helpful Hints

• Bananas that have darkened can be peeled and frozen in a plastic container until it's time to bake bread or cake.

• When bread is baking, a small dish of water in the oven will help to keep the crust from getting too hard or brown.

• Use shortening, not margarine or oil, to grease pans, as margarine and oil absorb more readily into the dough or batter and do not help to release baked goods from pan (especially bread).

• Use a metal ice tray divider to cut biscuits in a hurry. Press into dough and biscuits will separate at dividing lines when baked.

• Self-rising flour: 4 cups flour, 2 teaspoons salt and 2 tablespoons baking powder. Mix well and store in a tightly covered container.

• Hot water kills yeast. One way to tell the correct temperature is to pour the water over your forearm, and if you cannot feel either hot or cold, the temperature is just right.

• When in doubt, always sift flour before measuring.

• When cooking in glass pans, reduce oven temperature by 25 degrees.

• When milk is used in making bread, you get a finer texture. Water makes a coarser bread.

• To prevent scorching when scalding milk, first rinse pan in water.

• If your biscuits are dry, it could be from too much handling, or the oven temperature may not have been hot enough.

• Nut breads are better if stored 24 hours before using.

• To make bread crumbs, toast the heels of bread and put in blender or food processor.

• Cracked eggs should only be used in dishes that are thoroughly cooked; they may contain bacteria.

• The freshness of eggs can be tested by placing them in a large bowl of cold water; if they float, do not use them.

BREADS & ROLLS

APPLE-NUT MUFFINS

1¾ c. whole-wheat flour
1 tsp. cinnamon
1 c. buttermilk
⅓ c. oil
½ c. coarsely chopped nuts

2 med. diced apples with skin
2 tsp. baking soda
¼ tsp. nutmeg
1 egg
¼ c. honey

Add flour, soda, cinnamon, nutmeg to beaten buttermilk, egg, oil and honey. Stir in nuts and apples. Blend well. Put in muffin tins and bake at 400° for about 20 to 25 minutes. Makes 12.

Joan Pharis

BANANA-NUT BREAD

¾ c. butter
1⅓ c. mashed banana (3 med.)
1 tsp. vanilla
1 tsp. baking soda
½ c. butter or sour milk

1½ c. sugar
2 eggs, well beaten
2 c. flour
¾ tsp. salt
¾ c. chopped nuts

Cream butter and eggs thoroughly. Blend in bananas, eggs and vanilla. Sift flour, baking soda and salt together. Add banana mixture, alternating with buttermilk, mixing thoroughly after each addition. Add nuts and mix. Pour batter into greased and floured 9 x 5 x 3-inch loaf pan. Bake at 325° for 1¼ hours.

Connie Kinsel

BRAN MUFFINS

1½ c. bran
⅓ c. oil
1⅔ c. whole-wheat flour
1 T. baking powder
½ tsp. baking soda

1 c. skim milk
⅓ c. honey
2 eggs
½ tsp. salt

Preheat oven to 375°. Combine moist ingredients with bran; let stand 2 minutes. (If you let it stand much longer, the muffins turn out dry.) Add remaining ingredients, just stirring until combined. Spoon into paper-lined muffin cups. Bake 20 minutes or until done. Let cool a few minutes before serving so paper won't stick to muffin.

Cindi Rogers

BROCCOLI CORNBREAD

1 (10-oz.) pkg. frozen chopped
  broccoli
½ c. melted margarine
6 to 8 oz. cottage cheese

1 (7-oz.) pkg. cornbread mix
1 tsp. salt
4 eggs, beaten
1 med. chopped onion

Mix all together and bake in 10-inch nonstick pan for 30 minutes at 400°.

Beverly Gustafson

BUTTERMILK ROLLS

1 pkg. yeast
½ c. warm water (110°-115°)
2 T. butter or margarine
4 to 5 c. flour (can use whole-
  wheat & white flour)

1½ tsp. sugar
¼ c. honey
1½ c. buttermilk
1 tsp. salt

Dissolve yeast and sugar in warm water. Heat butter, honey and buttermilk until warm (110°-115°). Add to yeast mixture. Gradually add flour and knead until dough is smooth and elastic. Place in lightly greased bowl; cover and let rise until doubled in bulk, about 1 hour. Punch dough down and shape into rolls. Place in lightly greased pan(s). Cover and let rise until double. Bake at 350° for 12 to 15 minutes.

Alice Fritz Gerber

CHEESE ROLLS
(Like Pizzas)

1 lb. grated Tillamook cheese
  (med.)
1 sm. can chopped olives
1 (8-oz.) can tomato sauce

¼ c. chopped green pepper
¼ c. oil
1 garlic bud, cut fine

Combine all ingredients and chill. Can be spread on sliced sourdough French bread or split sourdough rolls. Bake at 350° for 15 minutes.

Dorothy Anderson

CLOCKWATCHER MUFFINS

5 c. sifted flour
5 tsp. cinnamon
1 (20-oz.) box raisin bran
1 qt. buttermilk
1 c. oil or melted shortening

5 tsp. baking soda
3 c. sugar
4 eggs, beaten
2 tsp. salt

Sift and measure flour. Sift flour with baking soda, cinnamon and salt. Mix in raisin bran and sugar. Add eggs, buttermilk and oil to dry ingredients. Mix until blended. Fill muffin tins ⅔ full. Bake at 400° for 20 minutes. Makes 5 dozen and batter may be stored in refrigerator up to 6 weeks. They also freeze well baked or raw.

Dorothy Anderson

COCONUT-BANANA CORNBREAD

1 c. yellow cornmeal
1 T. sugar
1¼ tsp. ground allspice
1 egg, beaten
¼ c. vegetable oil
½ c. sweetened flaked coconut

1 c. very ripe mashed bananas (2
  med.)
1 c. all-purpose flour
1 tsp. baking powder
¼ tsp. salt
¼ c. milk

Preheat oven to 325°. Grease an 8-inch square pan and set aside. In a medium bowl, combine dry ingredients. In another bowl combine egg, bananas, milk and

(continued)

oil. Form a well in center of dry ingredients. Add milk mixture all at once and stir just enough to combine. Stir in coconut. Pour mixture into greased pan. Bake in preheated oven about 25 minutes or until cake tester inserted in center comes out clean. Cut into 2-inch squares and serve hot with butter. Makes 16 squares. This recipe is from Kathleen Baty, Carolyn's niece in Menlo Park.

Carolyn Walter

DOUBLE CORNBREAD

1 c. flour
4 tsp. baking powder
2 T. sugar
6 oz. cheddar cheese, shredded
8½-oz. can cream-style corn
4-oz. can chopped green chilies

1 c. cornmeal
½ tsp. salt
⅓ c. milk
¼ c. oil
2 lg. eggs

Mix together and pour into greased pan. Bake 30 to 35 minutes at 400°.

Joyce O'Neal

EASY WHOLE-WHEAT BREAD

About 4⅓ c. whole-wheat flour
2 pkgs. active dry yeast
1¾ c. warm water (about 110°)
1½ tsp. salt

⅓ c. wheat germ
2 T. honey
¼ c. oil

Measure flour into bowl. Place bowl into warm oven (about 150°) until warmed through. In large bowl dissolve yeast and honey in ¾ cup of the water. Let stand about 15 minutes or until bubbly. Mix in remaining 1 cup water, oil and salt. Stir in wheat germ. Start adding flour, one cup at a time. Beat vigorously after each addition. When dough leaves sides of bowl, turn out on a floured surface and knead just enough to shape into a smooth loaf. Place loaf in greased 9 x 5-inch loaf pan and cover lightly with plastic wrap. Let rise 30 to 40 minutes in warm place, until about 1 inch above rim of pan. Bake in 400° oven for 35 minutes. Turn out on rack to cool.

Joan Pharis

MARIE CALENDAR CORNBREAD

3 eggs
1½ c. margarine, melted
⅔ c. sugar
2 tsp. baking powder

1¼ c. milk
2⅓ c. Bisquick
1 c. cornmeal

Mix all until blended. Pour into 9 x 13-inch pan. Bake at 350° for 30 minutes.

Joyce O'Neal

OAT PANCAKES

1 c. flour
½ c. oats, uncooked
1 c. skim milk
¼ c. egg substitute or 1 egg,
  beaten

1 T. baking powder
½ tsp. salt (opt.)
2 T. oil

Heat griddle on medium-high. Oil lightly. Combine dry ingredients. Add milk, egg and oil. Stir until dry ingredients are moistened. For each pancake, pour about ¼ cup batter on hot griddle. Turn when tops are covered with bubbles and edges look cooked. Turn only once. Serves 2 to 3.

Lori Pharis Wright

ORANGE COFFEECAKE

1 orange, ground
1 beaten egg
1 c. milk
½ c. oil
1 c. sugar

1 tsp. cinnamon
1 tsp. baking powder
1 tsp. soda
¼ tsp. nutmeg
2 c. flour

Sift all dry ingredients together. Add egg, milk, oil and ground-up orange to dry ingredients and mix. Pour batter into greased and floured 13 x 9-inch pan and top with following:

⅓ c. brown sugar
½ stick margarine or butter

1 c. chopped nuts

Mix together and put on top of batter in baking pan. Bake at 350° for 30 minutes.

Glaze:

¾ c. powdered sugar
1 T. milk

½ tsp. vanilla

Drizzle over cake while it is still warm.

Dorothy Anderson
An Ina Todd's Recipe

OVERNIGHT PULL-APART COFFEECAKE

1 pkg. Bridgeford frozen rolls
1 sm. pkg. regular butterscotch
  pudding (not instant)
½ c. chopped nuts

½ c. melted butter
½ c. brown sugar
2 tsp. cinnamon

Mix sugar, cinnamon and melted butter together and cool. Put frozen rolls in a well-greased bundt pan. Sprinkle with dry pudding and nuts. Pour melted butter mixture over rolls. Cover pan with waxed paper and towel. Place in cold oven overnight or about 8 hours, until dough has risen. Bake for 40 to 60 minutes at 325°. Turn upside down and serve warm.

Joan Pharis

23304-98

PARMESAN ROLLS

2 (¼-oz.) pkgs. active dry yeast
½ c. warm water (110°-115°)
1 c. warm milk (110°-115°)
½ c. grated Parmesan cheese
⅓ c. butter or margarine, melted

4½ to 5 c. all-purpose flour
2 eggs
1 c. cornmeal
1 tsp. salt
3 T. sugar

Topping:

1 c. butter or margarine, melted   ¼ c. grated Parmesan cheese

In a large mixing bowl, dissolve yeast in water. Add milk, Parmesan cheese, butter, sugar, salt, cornmeal and eggs and mix well. Add 3 cups of flour and beat until smooth. Add enough remaining flour to form a soft dough. Turn onto a floured board and knead until smooth and elastic, about 6 to 8 minutes. Place in a greased bowl, turning once to grease top. Cover and let rise in a warm place until doubled, about 1 hour. Punch dough down. Shape into 24 ovals and dip each into melted butter and Parmesan cheese. Place on greased baking sheets. Cover and let rise until doubled, about 30 minutes. Bake at 375° for 20 to 25 minutes or until golden brown. Remove from pans to cool on wire racks. Yields 2 dozen.

Erma Donaldson

PEAR-NUT BREAD

2 to 3 fresh Bartlett pears (can use
  canned)
½ c. oil
2 eggs
1 tsp. vanilla
½ tsp. salt
¼ tsp. cinnamon

½ c. chopped nuts
1 c. sugar
¼ c. sour cream
2 c. flour
1 tsp. soda
¼ tsp. nutmeg

Pare, halve and core pears. Chop to get 1 cup fruit. In large bowl, beat together oil and sugar. Beat in eggs, sour cream and vanilla. Sift together dry ingredients. Add oil-sugar mixture and continue to beat until well blended. Add nuts and pears; mix well. Spoon into well-greased 9 x 5-inch pan. Bake at 350° for 1 hour or until done. Let cool in pan for 10 to 15 minutes.

Marge Harward

PECAN-CRANBERRY MUFFINS

1½ to 2 c. chopped fresh or frozen
  cranberries
1¾ c. sugar, divided
3 c. all-purpose flour
4½ tsp. baking powder
½ tsp. salt
½ c. shortening (butter, margarine
  or Crisco)

2 eggs, slightly beaten
1 c. milk
1 c. chopped pecans
1 T. grated lemon peel (opt. - lemon
  juice)

In a bowl, toss chopped cranberries with ¾ cup sugar and set aside. Combine flour, baking powder, salt and remaining sugar. Cut in shortening until the mixture resembles coarse crumbs. Combine eggs and milk; stir into flour mixture just until

(continued)

moist. Fold in pecans, lemon peel and cranberries. Fill greased or paper-lined muffin cups ⅔ full. Bake at 400° for 20 to 25 minutes or until muffins test done.

Jean Edwards

ZUCCHINI BREAD

2 c. grated squash
3 eggs
1 c. oil
2 c. sugar
3 tsp. vanilla
1 c. chopped nuts

3 c. sifted flour
1 tsp. salt
1 tsp. soda
¼ tsp. baking powder
3 tsp. cinnamon

Beat eggs until light and foamy. Add oil, sugar, vanilla and grated squash. Mix lightly but well. Mix remaining ingredients and add to squash mixture. Pour into 2 well-greased 9 x 5 x 2-inch loaf pans or 4 small pans. Bake 1 hour at 325°. Remove from pans and cool on rack. Freezes well.

Susan Fiske

23304-98

Cakes,
Cookies
&
Candy

Helpful Hints

Child's Party:
• Push animal shaped cookie cutters lightly into icing. Fill depressed outlines with chocolate icing.
• Fill flat bottom ice cream cones with cake batter half full and bake. Decorate with icing topped with colored sugar.
• Small marshmallows can be used for candle holders on cakes.

Other Useful Tips:
• Spoon for Baby: The tablespoon from your measuring spoons set is ideal for babies to use when eating soup or cereal. The short handle and deep scoop helps them to get more into their mouths as they learn to feed themselves.

• Eliminating drink spills: Your child will be able to hold onto a glass better if you place two tight rubber bands around the glass an inch or so apart. This makes it easier for little hands to hold.

• To teach a child how to put the right shoe on the right foot, mark or tape the inside of the right shoe only.

• Has your child outgrown his favorite sweater? Don't throw it away. Chances are, it is only the sleeves that are too short. Cut off the sleeves and finish the armholes, and he will have a great sweater vest to wear.

• Want an inexpensive way to stretch your baby powder? Mix the baby powder with a box of cornstarch and it will go much further. Cornstarch is safe and will stretch your money also. Cornstarch is just fine to use alone.

• Want a good way to wean your baby from his or her bottle? Take the lid off the bottle and let the baby drink from the "old favorite" bottle, then start using a cup from there. Make sure you start with baby's favorite drink.

• Here is a good way to keep your baby's bottle warm when you go somewhere. After the baby's bottle is warmed, just pop it into a wide mouth thermos that has been "warmed" with hot water. Put on the lid. This will keep the bottle just right.

• Remember this simple tip when going to outings. A child in colorful clothes is easier to find. Nothing stands out in a crowd like a toddler in red, purple, or yellow.

• If your child has trouble swallowing a pill, place it in a teaspoon of applesauce and see how easily it goes down.

CAKES, COOKIES & CANDY

1-2-3-4 CAKE

1 c. margarine
3 c. flour
4 tsp. baking powder
1 c. milk
1 square chocolate

2 c. sugar
4 eggs
1½ tsp. vanilla
½ tsp. salt
Food coloring

Cream shortening and sugar. Add the eggs. Mix and sift flour, baking powder and salt. Add alternately with the milk. Other flavorings can be substituted. Divide batter into 3 parts. Add red food coloring to one until it is pink. Melt a square of chocolate in another part. Leave third one uncolored. Bake layers at 375° for 20 to 25 minutes. Our favorite for holidays!

Becky Burghardt
From F.C. Cookbook

APPLE CAKE

4 c. diced apples
2 c. sugar
1 tsp. nutmeg
1 c. chopped nuts
2 tsp. soda

2 eggs, unbeaten
2 tsp. cinnamon
½ c. oil
2 c. flour
1 tsp. salt

Glaze:

1 c. powdered sugar
1 to 2 T. milk

1 tsp. vanilla

Break eggs over apples. Add sugar, spices, oil and nuts. Mix well with a fork. Add flour, soda and salt. Mix with a fork. Pour into an 8½ x 13½-inch pan. Bake 45 minutes at 350°. Glaze hot from oven.

Ina Todd

CHOCOLATE-CHERRY CAKE

1 pkg. devil's food cake mix
21-oz. can cherry pie filling

1 tsp. almond flavoring
2 eggs, beaten

Mix together and pour into greased 9 x 13-inch pan. Bake 25 to 30 minutes at 350°.

Frosting:

1 c. sugar
6 oz. semi-sweet chocolate chips

5 T. margarine
⅓ c. milk

In small pan, combine sugar, margarine and milk and boil for 1 minute, stirring constantly. Remove from heat and stir in chips until smooth. Pour over warm cake.

Fronia Campbell

CHRISTMAS CRUMB CAKE

2 c. flour	1 c. sour milk
2 c. brown sugar	½ tsp. cinnamon
⅔ c. shortening	½ tsp. nutmeg
½ tsp. salt	½ tsp. soda
2 tsp. baking powder	Almonds or walnuts, chopped
2 eggs, beaten	

Rub together flour, sugar, salt and shortening until crumbly. Take ½ cup crumbs to sprinkle on top. To remainder, add spices and baking powder. Beat soda and sour milk together, then mix with eggs. Stir into dry mixture. Spread into 2 well-greased layer cake pans or large-sized Pyrex dish. To the ½ cup crumbs, add some almonds or walnuts. Sprinkle this on top of batter. Bake at 400° for 10 minutes, then reduce to 350° for 15 minutes. Keeps moist for days. Freezes well. Always better if heated again before serving. The Walters use this recipe throughout the year.

Mildred Walters

CRAZY CAKE

Use a 9 x 13-inch pan. Sift together and mix in pan with a fork:

3 c. flour	2 c. sugar
½ c. cocoa	2 tsp. salt
1 tsp. salt	

Add and mix thoroughly with fork:

⅔ c. oil	2 tsp. vanilla
2 T. vinegar	2 c. water

Bake 30 to 35 minutes at 350°.

Topping:

½ c. butter	1 c. sugar
½ c. milk	1 T. flour
½ tsp. vanilla	1 c. chopped walnuts

Cook until thick; cool and pour over cake.

Joan Pharis

CREAM CAKE

⅔ c. shortening	2 c. sugar
2 eggs	2 tsp. vanilla
2 c. cream	2 c. flour
3 tsp. baking powder	1 tsp. salt

Mix together and pour into 9 x 13-inch greased and floured pan. Bake at 350° for 35 minutes. This is great for Strawberry Shortcake!

Joyce O'Neal

23304-98

CINNAMON SUPPER CAKE

¾ c. sugar
1 egg
½ c. milk
1½ tsp. baking powder
1 T. soft butter
1 tsp. cinnamon

¼ c. shortening
1 tsp. vanilla
1 c. flour
¼ tsp. salt
3 T. powdered sugar

Gradually beat sugar to shortening and cream until fluffy. Beat egg and add vanilla and milk. Sift together flour, baking powder, salt. Add to egg mixture and stir until smooth. Bake in greased 9-inch pan at 375° for 20 to 25 minutes. Immediately spread top with soft butter. Sift the powdered sugar with cinnamon. Sprinkle over top of cake. Serve while warm.

Dorothy Anderson

DRIED FRUIT CAKE

1 (8-oz.) pkg. pitted dates
2 c. quartered dried apricots
1½ c. almond pieces
1½ c. walnut pieces
1 c. golden raisins

¾ c. sugar
¾ c. flour
3 eggs
Rum or brandy (opt.)

Butter a 5 x 9-inch loaf pan; line with waxed paper, then butter paper. In a large bowl, combine fruits and nuts. Stir together flour, sugar and baking powder to blend. Add to fruit and nut mixture. Beat eggs with vanilla to blend. Stir thoroughly to blend with fruit mixture. Spoon batter into loaf pan; spread evenly, pressing batter into corners of pan. Bake at 300° until golden brown, about 2 hours. Start checking with knife after 1 hour. I never bake it for 2! Cool in pan on wire rack for 10 minutes, then turn out of pan. Peel off paper and cool on rack. Wrap in foil. Chill at least 2 days or up to 2 months. If desired, sprinkle top of cake with 1 tablespoon rum or brandy once a week.

Joanne Carter

ITALIAN CREAM CAKE

1 c. buttermilk
2 c. sugar
½ c. shortening
1 c. chopped nuts
1 cube margarine

1 tsp. soda
5 eggs, separated
1 tsp. vanilla
1 (4-oz.) can coconut
2 c. flour

Combine soda and buttermilk; let stand. Cream sugar, margarine and shortening. Add egg yolks, one at a time, beating well. Add buttermilk and flour to creamed mixture. Beat egg whites gently. Stir in egg whites, nuts and coconut. Bake in 2 (9-inch) pans at 325° for 30 minutes or until it tests done. Ice with cream cheese icing.

Opal Williams

KLAN APPLE KAKE

4 to 5 diced apples (about 4 c.)   2 lg. eggs
1 tsp. soda   2 c. flour
1/4 tsp. salt   2 c. sugar
1/2 c. salad oil   2 tsp. cinnamon
1 c. chopped nuts

Put apples in large mixing bowl. Add eggs, sugar and mix. Do not overblend. Add flour and other ingredients. Blend with a wooden spoon. Add chopped nuts. **Do not** use mixer - blend just enough to mix all. **Do not** mash apples. Bake at 325° for 1 hour (or until done) in a 9 x 12-inch Pyrex pan. Ice lightly or serve with ice cream or whipped cream.

Judy Burtoft

LAZY DAISY CAKE

4 eggs   1/4 c. butter (margarine)
2 tsp. vanilla extract   2 c. sugar
2 tsp. baking powder   2 c. all-purpose flour
1 c. milk   1/2 tsp. salt

Frosting

1 1/2 c. packed brown sugar   2 c. flaked coconut
3/4 c. butter (margarine), melted   1/2 c. half & half

In mixing bowl, beat eggs, sugar and vanilla until thick, about 4 minutes. Combine flour, baking powder and salt. Add to egg mixture and beat just until combined. In a saucepan, bring milk and butter to a boil, stirring constantly. Add to batter and beat until combined. Pour into a greased 13 x 9 x 2-inch baking pan. Bake at 350° for 35 to 40 minutes or until cake tests done. Combine frosting ingredients. Spread over warm cake. Broil until lightly browned, about 3 to 4 minutes. Yields 16 to 20 servings.

Erma Donaldson

LEMON ANGEL CAKE

1 baked 10-inch angel food cake   3/4 c. sugar
1 T. unflavored gelatin   3/4 c. lemon juice
6 egg yolks, beaten   6 egg whites
1 1/2 tsp. grated lemon peel   3/4 c. sugar
1/4 c. cold water   1 c. heavy cream, whipped

Soften gelatin in cold water. Combine egg yolks, sugar, lemon peel and juice. Cook over boiling water, stirring constantly, until mixture coats spoon. Remove from heat and add softened gelatin, stirring until dissolved. Cook until partially set. Beat egg whites until foamy. Gradually beat in sugar and continue to beat until stiff and glossy. Fold into custard. Remove crusts from angel cake. Tear cake into pieces. Half fill a buttered 10-inch tube or 9 x 13-inch pan with cake pieces. Add filling and the rest of cake pieces, pushing down into filling. Chill until firm. Frost with whipped cream or whipped topping.

Mildred Walters

23304-98

LEMON POUND CAKE

3-oz. box lemon Jello
1 box lemon cake mix (Duncan Hines)
¾ c. water

1 lemon rind, grated
¾ c. oil
4 eggs

Combine all ingredients and beat until smooth. Pour into greased and floured 9 x 13-inch baking dish. Bake at 350° for 40 to 45 minutes. Prick all over top with fork and cover with glaze while warm. **Glaze:** Two cups powdered sugar blended with juice of 2 fresh lemons. Easy, good and keeps well!

Dorothy Anderson

MOM'S CARROT CAKE

2 c. flour
2 tsp. soda
1 sm. can crushed pineapple
2 c. grated carrots
1½ tsp. salt
1 c. chopped nuts

1½ c. oil
2 tsp. cinnamon
2 tsp. vanilla
3 eggs
2 c. sugar
1 pkg. coconut

Cream sugar and oil. Add all remaining ingredients. Pour into greased and floured 13 x 9-inch pan. Bake at 350° for 35 to 40 minutes.

Buttermilk Frosting:

1 c. sugar
½ stick butter
½ c. buttermilk

1 T. white Karo syrup
½ tsp. soda
½ tsp. vanilla

Mix all ingredients except vanilla in saucepan. Bring to a boil and cook 5 minutes, stirring constantly. Remove from stove and add vanilla. Pour immediately over cake.

Kathie Gifford

PINEAPPLE SHEETCAKE

2 eggs
2 tsp. soda
Dash salt
½ c. chopped nuts
2½ c. (20-oz. can) undrained crushed pineapple

2 c. flour
2 c. sugar
1 tsp. vanilla

Mix all ingredients together. Pour into greased jellyroll pan (15 x 11 x 2 inches). Bake at 350° for 20 to 25 minutes. While warm, spread the following:

1 (3-oz.) pkg. cream cheese
1¾ c. powdered sugar

1 tsp. vanilla
¼ c. margarine

Blend above; spread on warm cake and sprinkle with ½ cup chopped nuts.

Dorothy Anderson

PISTACHIO CAKE

1 pkg. yellow cake mix	3 eggs
1 pkg. pistachio instant pudding	1 c. oil
1 c. club soda	½ c. chopped nuts

Mix all together and beat for 2 minutes. Pour into 9 x 13-inch greased pan. Bake at 350° for 40 minutes.

Icing:

1 pkg. instant pistachio pudding	1 c. milk
1 (8-oz.) ctn. Cool Whip	

Mix milk and pudding. Add Cool Whip. Frost cake when cool. Simple and just too good!

Carolyn Walter

PISTACHIO-CHOCOLATE CHIP CUPCAKES

1¾ c. flour	⅔ c. sugar
1 (4 serving size) pistachio instant pudding	2 eggs, beaten
	½ tsp. salt
2½ tsp. baking powder	1¼ c. milk
¾ c. miniature chocolate chip pieces	1 tsp. vanilla
	Cream Cheese Frosting
½ c. cooking oil	

In large mixing bowl, stir together dry ingredients. In small bowl combine beaten eggs, milk, oil and vanilla. Stir into flour mixture just until combined. Full muffin cups ⅔ full. Bake at 375° for 18 to 20 minutes. Frost when cooled.

Joyce O'Neal

PUMPKIN SHEETCAKE

1 (16-oz.) can pumpkin	2 c. sugar
1 c. vegetable oil	4 eggs, lightly beaten
2 c. all-purpose flour	2 tsp. baking soda
1 tsp. ground cinnamon	½ tsp. salt

Frosting:

1 (3-oz.) pkg. cream cheese, softened	1¾ c. powdered sugar
	3 to 4 tsp. milk
5 T. butter (margarine)	Chopped nuts
1 tsp. vanilla extract	

In a mixing bowl, beat pumpkin, sugar and oil. Add eggs and mix well. Combine flour, baking soda, cinnamon and salt. Add to pumpkin mixture and beat until well blended. Pour into a greased 15 x 10 x 1-inch baking pan. Bake at 350° for 25 to 30 minutes or until cake tests done. Cool. Beat cream cheese, butter and vanilla in a mixing bowl until smooth. Gradually add sugar and mix well. Add milk until

(continued)

23304-98

frosting reaches desired spreading consistency. Frost cake. Sprinkle with nuts. Yields 20 to 24 servings.

Erma Donaldson

QUICK PUMPKIN CAKE

1 can pumpkin pie mix
1 pkg. yellow cake mix

2 cubes melted margarine
1 c. chopped nuts

Follow directions on pumpkin pie mix can. Put in 2 x 9 x 13-inch dish. Spread yellow cake mix evenly over pumpkin. Drip melted margarine from spoon evenly over dry cake mix. Sprinkle chopped nuts on top. Bake at 350° for 1 hour or when testing shows done.

Emma Geren

SCRIPTURE CAKE

This is an ancient sort of fruit cake. It was used for weddings, baptisms and funerals. No one knows who came up with the original recipe or just how long it has been used.

4½ c. 1st Kings 4:22
1 c. Judges 5:25
2 c. Jeremiah 6:20
2 c. 1st Samuel 30:12
2 c. Nahum 3:12
2 c. Numbers 17:8

2 T. 1st Samuel 14:25
½ tsp. Leviticus 2:13
½ c. Judges 4:19
2 T. Amos 4:25
6 med. Jeremiah 17:11

Find the ingredients in the Scriptures and measure them out. Mix all ingredients. Place in loaf pan or cake pan, greased and floured or lined. Bake slowly (300°) for about an hour or more. The original was most likely baked in outdoor (or brick) ovens so you may have to experiment with the time.

Toni Williams

BROWN SUGAR SQUARES

1 c. shortening (half Crisco & half butter)
1 c. dark brown sugar
1 unbeaten egg yolk (save white)
1 tsp. vanilla

2 c. flour
Dash salt
1 tsp. cinnamon
½ c. chopped nuts

Cream shortening and sugar. Add other ingredients except nuts. Pat out thin on well-greased cookie sheet. Spread unbeaten egg white on top. Sprinkle on the chopped nuts. Bake 40 minutes in slow oven (275°-300°). Cut into small rectangles while still hot. Let cool to become crisp. Good served cold.

Mildred Walters

BROWNIE-NUT SLICES

2 sticks (1 c.) butter or margarine
  (not spread), softened
1¼ c. sugar
½ tsp. baking soda
1 lg. egg
2 c. all-purpose flour

½ c. unsweetened cocoa powder
½ c. semi-sweet chocolate mini
  chips
½ c. walnuts, finely chopped,
  spread on waxed paper

Beat butter, sugar and baking soda in a large bowl with an electric mixer until fluffy. Beat in egg. With mixer on low speed, beat in flour and cocoa, half at a time, until blended. Stir in chocolate chips. Divide dough in half. Roll each half on a lightly floured surface into 7-inch log. Roll in nuts until logs are 10 inches long. Wrap each in plastic wrap. Refrigerate at least 14 hours, until firm, or up to 1 week. Heat oven to 350°. Cut logs in ½-inch slices. Place 1 inch apart on greased cookie sheet(s). Bake 8 to 10 minutes, just until set and tops look dry. Let cool a few minutes before removing to racks to cool. Store airtight. Makes 40.

Carolyn Walter

BUTTERMILK BROWNIES

Mix:

2 c. flour
2 c. sugar

1 tsp. soda

Mix and bring to a boil:

2 cubes margarine
2 T. cocoa

1 c. water

Add hot mixture to dry mixture. Add:

2 eggs
⅓ c. buttermilk

1 tsp. vanilla

Bake in greased only jellyroll pan at 400° for 10 minutes.

Frosting (bring to boil):

1 cube margarine
5 T. buttermilk

4 T. cocoa

Add 1 pound powdered sugar. Frost while warm.

Dorothy Anderson

BEE STING BARS

In a small pan combine:

½ c. butter
3 T. honey
2 T. canned milk

¼ c. sugar
1 c. sliced or slivered almonds

Bring ingredients to a boil over medium heat, stirring constantly, until it reaches a rolling boil. Set mixture aside. In a mixing bowl stir together:

(continued)

18

23304-98

1¾ c. flour
½ c. sugar

2 tsp. baking powder
¼ tsp. salt

Cut ½ cup butter into small pieces and add to flour using a pastry blender or 2 knives. Cut butter into flour until no large pieces remain and mixture is very crumbly. Beat 1 egg with 1 teaspoon vanilla and 2 teaspoons water. Pour into flour mixture and mix with a fork until dough holds together. Using your hands, press dough evenly in bottom of an ungreased 10 x 15-inch baking pan. Pour almond mixture over the dough, spreading evenly. Bake in 350° oven for 20 to 25 minutes, until top is deep golden brown. Let cool in pan and cut into bars. Store airtight.

Carolyn Walter

BUTTERMILK COOKIES WITH FROSTING

1 c. shortening
2 c. sugar
2 eggs
1 c. buttermilk
1½ tsp. vanilla

5 c. flour
½ tsp. salt
2 tsp. baking powder
2 tsp. soda

Cream shortening, sugar and vanilla. Add buttermilk. Sift dry ingredients and add, mixing well. Drop by tablespoon on ungreased cookie sheet. Bake at 350° for 10 minutes.

Frosting:

¼ lb. butter or margarine
1-lb. box powdered sugar
¼ tsp. salt

¼ c. milk (buttermilk is OK)
1 tsp. vanilla

Mix until smooth and use to frost cooled cookies.

Dorothy Anderson

CEREAL SNAPS

½ c. butter or margarine
½ c. brown sugar
½ c. granulated sugar
1 egg
1 tsp. vanilla
1¼ c. sifted flour

½ tsp. baking soda
½ tsp. baking powder
½ tsp. salt
2 c. Rice Krispies
1⅓ c. coconut

Cream butter with brown sugar and granulated sugar. Add egg and vanilla, creaming until light and fluffy. Sift together flour, baking soda, baking powder and salt. Stir together with creamed mixture. Stir in Rice Krispies and coconut. Shape into ¾-inch balls and place on ungreased cookie sheet, pressing down lightly with fork. Bake at 350° for 10 minutes or until lightly brown. Cool slightly before removing from pan.

Ina Todd

CHEESECAKE COOKIES

⅓ c. butter
⅓ c. brown sugar
1 c. flour
½ c. chopped nuts
¼ c. white sugar

8 oz. cream cheese
1 egg
2 T. lemon juice
½ tsp. vanilla

Cream brown sugar and butter in small bowl. Add flour and nuts to make crumb mixture (reserve 1 cup for topping). Press remaining into 8 x 8-inch pan. Bake at 350° for 12 to 15 minutes, until lightly brown. Blend white sugar and cream cheese. Add egg, lemon juice and vanilla. Beat well. Spread over baked crust. Sprinkle with reserved crumbs. Bake at 340° for 25 minutes. Cool; cut into small squares.

Mildred Walters

CHINESE ALMOND COOKIES

1 c. softened margarine
1 c. sugar
2 eggs
¼ c. light Karo syrup
2 T. almond extract

3¾ c. sifted flour
1½ tsp. baking soda
1 c. whole blanched shelled
  almonds
2 T. water

Heat oven to 350°. Beat margarine, sugar and 1 egg together until light and fluffy. Blend in Karo and almond extract. Combine dry ingredients and blend into shortening mixture. Chill dough. Pinch off small pieces about size of walnut and form into a ball. Place 2 inches apart on cookie sheet. Flatten each with palm of hand to ¼ inch thick. Press almond into center. Beat remaining egg with water and brush onto cookie for shiny glaze. Bake 12 to 15 minutes or until golden brown. Cool. Makes 8 dozen cookies.

Dorothy Anderson

CHOCOLATE CHIP-NUT BARS

2 c. sifted cake flour
1 tsp. baking powder
½ tsp. salt
¼ tsp. baking soda
2 pkgs. semi-sweet chocolate chips

2 c. chopped walnuts
2 c. brown sugar
2 eggs, slightly beaten
2 tsp. vanilla
⅔ c. shortening

Sift flour, baking powder, salt, soda together twice. Cream together until light and fluffy: shortening and sugar. Add eggs and vanilla and mix well. Add flour mixture gradually, mixing well after each addition. Add chocolate chips and nuts; blend. Turn mixture into greased 11 x 15-inch pan. Bake in moderate (350°) oven for 25 to 30 minutes. Cut into bars 1¾ x 2¼ inches. Remove from pan and cool on cake rack. Makes about 40 bars.

Alice Anderson

23304-98

CHOCOLATE MALTED COOKIES

1 c. butter-flavored shortening
1¼ c. packed brown sugar
½ c. malted milk powder
2 T. chocolate syrup
1 T. vanilla extract
1½ c. semi-sweet chocolate chunks

1 c. (6 oz.) milk chocolate chips
1 egg
2 c. all-purpose flour
1 tsp. baking soda
½ tsp. salt

In a mixing bowl, combine shortening, brown sugar, milk powder, chocolate syrup and vanilla extract and beat for 2 minutes. Add egg. Combine the flour, baking soda and salt. Gradually add to creamed mixture, mixing well after each addition. Stir in chocolate chunks and chips. Shape into 2-inch balls and place 3 inches apart on ungreased baking sheets. Bake at 375° for 12 to 15 minutes or until golden brown. Cool for 2 minutes before removing to a wire rack. Makes about 1½ dozen.

Erma Donaldson

COCONUT WASHBOARDS

½ c. butter or margarine, softened
2 c. packed brown sugar
¼ c. water
4 c. all-purpose flour
1½ tsp. baking powder
½ tsp. baking soda

1 c. flaked coconut
½ c. shortening
2 eggs
1 tsp. vanilla extract
⅓ tsp. salt

In a mixing bowl, cream butter, shortening and sugar for 2 minutes or until fluffy. Add eggs; mix well. Gradually add water and vanilla; mix well. Combine flour, baking powder, baking soda and salt. Add to the creamed mixture. Fold in coconut. Cover and refrigerate for 2 to 4 hours. Shape into 1-inch balls. Place 2 inches apart on greased baking sheets; flatten with fingers into 2½ x 1-inch oblong shapes. Press lengthwise with a floured fork. Bake at 400° for 8 to 10 minutes or until lightly browned. Cool 2 minutes before removing to a wire rack. Makes about 9 dozen.

Erma Donaldson

CHOCOLATY DOUBLE CRUNCHERS

½ c. butter or margarine, softened
½ c. packed brown sugar
½ tsp. vanilla extract
½ tsp. baking soda
1 c. quick-cooking oats
1 c. crushed cornflakes

½ c. flaked coconut
½ c. sugar
1 egg
1 c. all-purpose flour
¼ tsp. salt

Filling:

2 (3-oz.) pkgs. cream cheese,
  softened
1½ c. confectioners' sugar

2 c. (12 oz.) semi-sweet chocolate
  chips, melted

In a mixing bowl, cream butter and sugars. Add egg and vanilla; mix well. Combine flour, baking soda and salt. Add to creamed mixture and mix well. Add oats,

(continued)

cornflakes and coconut. Shape into 1-inch balls and place 2 inches apart on greased baking sheets. Flatten with a glass dipped lightly in flour. Bake at 350° for 8 to 10 minutes or until lightly browned. Remove to wire racks to cool. **Filling:** Beat cream cheese and sugar until smooth. Add the chocolate; mix well. Spread about 1 tablespoon on half of the cookies and top each with another cookie. Store in the refrigerator. Makes about 2 dozen.

Erma Donaldson

CINNAMON CRUNCH BARS

12 cinnamon graham crackers
2 c. finely chopped walnuts
1 c. butter or margarine

1 c. firmly packed brown sugar
¼ tsp. ground cinnamon

Preheat oven to 400°. Arrange crackers in a single layer with sides touching in bottom of a greased 10 x 15-inch jellyroll pan. Sprinkle walnuts over crackers. In heavy small saucepan, combine butter, brown sugar and cinnamon, stirring constantly. Cook over medium heat until sugar dissolves and mixture begins to boil. Boil syrup 3 minutes longer without stirring. Pour over crackers. Bake 8 to 10 minutes, until bubbly and slightly darker around the edges. Cool completely. Break into pieces. Store in tight container. Makes about 1¼ dozen.

Betty Lynn

COOKIE DOUGH BROWNIES

2 c. sugar
½ c. all-purpose flour
½ c. baking cocoa
1 c. vegetable oil

2 tsp. vanilla extract
½ c. chopped walnuts (opt.)
½ tsp. salt
4 eggs

Filling:

½ c. butter or margarine, softened
½ c. packed brown sugar
¼ c. sugar

2 T. milk
1 tsp. vanilla extract
1 c. all-purpose flour

Glaze:

1 c. (6 oz.) semi-sweet chocolate
   chips

1 T. shortening
¾ c. chopped walnuts

In a mixing bowl, combine sugar, flour, cocoa and salt. Add oil, eggs and vanilla; beat at medium speed for 3 minutes. Stir in walnuts, if desired. Pour into a greased 13 x 9 x 2-inch baking pan. Bake at 350° for 30 minutes or until brownies test done. Cool completely. **Filling:** Cream butter and sugars in a mixing bowl. Add milk and vanilla; mix well. Beat in flour. Spread over the brownies. Chill until firm. **Glaze:** Melt chocolate chips and shortening in a saucepan, stirring until smooth. Spread over filling. Immediately sprinkle with nuts, pressing down slightly. Makes 3 dozen.

Erma Donaldson

22

COWBOY COOKIES

1 c. margarine
1 c. white sugar
1 tsp. vanilla
1 tsp. soda
2 c. oatmeal
1 c. walnuts (lg. pieces)
½ c. coconut

1 c. brown sugar
2 eggs
2 c. flour
1 tsp. baking powder
1 c. chocolate bits
½ c. raisins

Cream margarine, sugars and vanilla together. Add eggs and vanilla to creamed mixture. Mix flour, soda and baking powder. Add dry ingredients to creamed mixture and blend. Add oatmeal, chocolate bits, walnuts, raisins and coconut; mix. Put on greased cookie sheet and bake for 10 to 12 minutes at 375°.

Susan Fiske

CRANBERRY-DATE BARS

1 (12-oz.) bag fresh or frozen
   cranberries
1 (8-oz.) pkg. chopped dates
2 c. all-purpose flour
2 c. old-fashioned oats
1½ c. packed brown sugar

1 c. butter or margarine, melted
1 tsp. vanilla extract
½ tsp. salt
½ tsp. baking soda
2 T. water

Glaze:

2 c. confectioners' sugar
2 to 3 T. orange juice

½ tsp. vanilla extract

In a covered saucepan over low heat, simmer cranberries, dates and water for 15 minutes, stirring occasionally, until the cranberries have popped. Remove from the heat. Stir in vanilla and set aside. In a large bowl, combine the flour, oats, brown sugar, baking soda and salt. Stir in butter until well blended. Pat half into an ungreased 13 x 9 x 2-inch baking pan. Bake at 350° for 8 minutes. Spoon cranberry mixture over crust. Sprinkle with the remaining oat mixture. Pat gently. Bake at 350° for 24 to 30 minutes or until browned. Cool. Combine glaze ingredients; drizzle over bars. Makes 3 dozen.

Erma Donaldson

DELICIOUS COOKIES

1 c. oil
1 c. margarine
1 egg
1 c. coconut &/or nuts
3½ c. flour
1 tsp. salt (opt.)
2 tsp. vanilla

1 c. white sugar
1 c. brown sugar
1 c. Rice Krispies
1 c. oatmeal
1 tsp. soda
1 tsp. cream of tartar

(continued)

Blend oil, margarine and sugars. Add egg and beat well. Add rest of ingredients. Roll into balls and press down with glass dipped in granulated sugar or add a little cinnamon to this sugar. Bake at 350° for 8 to 10 minutes. Makes 8 dozen.

Marge Todd

DOWN SOUTH BARS

2 T. butter or margarine	2 eggs
1 c. chopped nuts	1 c. brown sugar
5 T. flour	$\frac{1}{8}$ tsp. soda

Melt butter in 8 x 8-inch pan. Beat eggs. Combine sugar, flour, soda and nuts. Stir into eggs. Add vanilla. Pour over melted butter. **Do not stir.** Bake 20 minutes at 350°. Let cool. Slice and roll in powdered sugar.

Toni Williams

DREAM BARS

1 c. flour	$\frac{1}{2}$ c. butter
$\frac{1}{2}$ c. brown sugar	

Mix until crumbly; pat into buttered pan. Bake at 350° for 15 minutes, until slightly browned.

1 c. brown sugar	2 eggs
1 tsp. vanilla	2 T. flour
$\frac{1}{2}$ tsp. baking powder	$\frac{1}{4}$ tsp. salt
$1\frac{1}{2}$ c. coconut	1 c. nuts

Mix together and pour over baked mixture above. Bake at 350° for 20 to 25 minutes or until brown. When cool, cut in bars.

Mildred Walters

E Z COOKIES

1 cake mix (any kind)	2 eggs
$\frac{1}{3}$ c. cooking oil or 1 c. oleo	

Mix well and bake at 350° for 10 to 12 minutes in shallow pan. For variety, add one or more of the following: raisins, nuts, rolled oats, spices or grated lemon peel.

Fronia Campbell

FROSTED CHOCOLATE COOKIES

Beat together:

1 c. brown sugar	1 egg & 1 egg yolk or $\frac{3}{4}$ c. egg
$\frac{1}{2}$ c. butter or margarine	substitute

Sift together:

$1\frac{1}{2}$ c. flour	$\frac{1}{4}$ tsp. salt
1 tsp. soda	

(continued)

23304-98

Add flour mixture to creamed mixture alternating with ½ cup milk. Add:

2 squares chocolate, melted (or 6 T. cocoa)
1 c. dates, chopped

1 c. nuts, chopped
1 tsp. vanilla

Bake at 350° for 12 minutes. **Original Frosting:** Beat the extra egg white with 1 tablespoon water. Add 1 cup sifted powdered sugar, 1 square melted chocolate or 3 tablespoons cocoa and 1 teaspoon vanilla.

Becky Burghardt

FROSTED GINGER COOKIES

1½ c. butter or margarine
1 c. packed brown sugar
½ c. molasses
4½ c. all-purpose flour
2 tsp. baking soda
2 tsp. ground cinnamon

1 c. sugar
2 eggs
2 tsp. vanilla extract
1 tsp. ground ginger
½ tsp. salt
½ tsp. ground cloves

Frosting:

⅓ c. packed brown sugar
2 c. confectioners' sugar
2 T. butter or margarine

½ tsp. vanilla or caramel flavoring
¼ c. milk
Pinch salt

In a mixing bowl, cream butter and sugars. Add the eggs, one at a time, beating well after each addition. Stir in molasses and vanilla; mix well. Combine dry ingredients. Gradually add to creamed mixture. Drop by tablespoonfuls 2 inches apart onto ungreased baking sheets. Bake at 325° for 12 to 15 minutes or until cookies spring back when touched lightly (do not overbake). Remove to wire racks. **Frosting:** In a medium saucepan, bring sugars and butter to a boil; boil for 1 minute, stirring constantly. Remove from the heat (mixture will look curdled at first). Cool for 3 minutes. Add vanilla and salt; mix well. Frost warm cookies. Makes about 6 dozen.

Erma Donaldson

FROZEN COOKIES

1 c. brown sugar
1 c. white sugar
¾ c. butter
½ tsp. salt
3 eggs
1 tsp. vanilla

2 T. milk
1 tsp. cinnamon
1 tsp. soda
5½ c. flour
½ lb. walnuts
½ lb. dates

Mix dough and roll into long rolls. Leave in refrigerator several days before baking. Cut into ⅓-inch thick slices and bake for 10 to 12 minutes in moderate oven (350°). This recipe is approximately 70 years old. It is from my mother's file.

Marge Todd

GRANDMA'S OATMEAL COOKIES

2 c. sugar
2 c. shortening
2 c. quick oats
1 tsp. cinnamon
½ tsp. soda
2 eggs
½ c. milk

2 c. flour
½ tsp. nutmeg
¼ tsp. cloves
1 c. raisins (opt.)
1 c. chocolate chips (opt.)
1 c. chopped nuts (opt.)

Mix together sugar, eggs and shortening with spoon. When thoroughly mixed, add other ingredients, mixing well after each addition. Bake 12 to 15 minutes at 375°-400°. If you want thinner cookies after you bake the first batch, add more milk; if you want thicker cookies, add more flour. Makes 5 to 6 dozen.

Nancy Anderson

HAMPSHIRE SOUR CREAM-GINGER SQUARES

1 c. butter
½ c. sugar
1 tsp. ginger
3½ c. sifted cake flour
2 tsp. baking soda

1 c. light molasses
½ c. sour cream
1 tsp. cinnamon
1 egg, beaten
¾ tsp. salt

Cream butter with sugar and spices. Combine beaten egg, molasses and sour cream. Sift together flour, soda and salt. Add alternately with molasses mixture to creamed butter and sugar. Spread in greased, shallow baking pan (15½ x 10½ x 1 inch). Bake in moderate (350°) oven for 20 minutes. Cool in pan. Frost with sour cream frosting. Cut into 2-inch squares.

Frosting:

1 c. sour cream
2 T. brown sugar or maple syrup

Dash cinnamon

Blend gently and chill before serving. Makes about 3 dozen.

Julia Stevens

HAZELNUT SHORTBREAD

1 c. butter, softened (no substitute)
2 T. maple syrup or honey
2 c. all-purpose flour
1¼ c. hazelnuts or filberts, finely
  chopped

½ c. semi-sweet chocolate chips
½ c. sugar
2 tsp. vanilla extract

In a mixing bowl, cream butter and sugar. Add syrup and vanilla. Add flour and mix just until combined. Fold in the nuts. Shape into 2 (1½-inch) rolls and wrap tightly in waxed paper. Chill for 2 hours or until firm. Cut into ¼-inch slices and place 2 inches apart on ungreased baking sheets. Bake at 325° for 14 to 16 minutes or until edges begin to brown. Remove to wire racks to cool. Melt chocolate chips; drizzle over cookies. Allow chocolate to harden. Makes about 6 dozen.

Erma Donaldson

23304-98

HOLIDAY CHOCOLATE BUTTER COOKIES

½ c. sugar
¾ c. butter, softened
1 egg yolk

1 tsp. almond extract
1½ c. all-purpose flour
¼ c. unsweetened cocoa

Heat oven to 375°. In a large bowl combine all ingredients except flour and cocoa. Beat at medium speed until light and fluffy, 2 to 3 minutes. Gradually add flour and cocoa until well mixed, 2 to 3 minutes. Shape rounded teaspoon as desired (1-inch balls will flatten to 2 or 3 inches). Flatten or use cookie press. Bake for 7 to 9 minutes or until set. Cool. Decorate with melted chocolate chips, dates, nuts, colored sugar, maraschino cherries, etc. Makes about 3 dozen.

Linda Dungan

ICEBOX CINNAMON COOKIES

3½ c. flour
1 tsp. baking soda
1 T. cinnamon
¼ tsp. salt
1 c. finely chopped nuts

1 c. brown sugar
1 c. granulated sugar
2 eggs
1 c. butter

Sift flour, baking soda, cinnamon and salt together. Work butter until soft. Work in sugars until smooth. Mix in dry ingredients. Add nuts last. Make into rolls; wrap in waxed paper and chill. Slice and bake at 350° for 10 to 12 minutes. Good recipe when you need **a lot**!

Dorothy Anderson

JUMBO COOKIES

12 eggs
2 lbs. brown sugar
4 c. white sugar
1 lb. butter or margarine
15 to 16 c. quick oats
1 lb. M & M's

1 T. vanilla
1 T. Karo syrup
8 tsp. baking soda
3 lbs. peanut butter
1 lb. chocolate chips

In a super large bowl, mix all ingredients together. Drop by ice cream scoop onto cookie sheet. Bake at 350° for 9 to 10 minutes.

Barbara Lockridge

LEMON BARS

Combine:

1 c. butter
2 c. flour

½ c. powdered sugar

Put into 9 x 13-inch pan and bake 15 minutes at 350°. Combine:

2 c. sugar
4 T. flour
1 tsp. baking powder

4 eggs, beaten
6 T. lemon juice

(continued)

Spread mixture over crust and bake for 25 minutes at 350°. When ready to serve, dust with powdered sugar.

Linda Anderson
Via Her Aunt Betty Baird

LEMON BITES

1 (18.25-oz.) pkg. lemon-flavored
  cake mix
14-oz. ctn. frozen nondairy whipped
  topping, thawed

½ c. sifted confectioners' sugar
1 egg

Preheat oven to 350°. In a large bowl, combine cake mix, egg and topping (batter will be very stiff). Drop teaspoons of dough into powdered sugar. Roll into 1-inch balls using sugar to keep dough from sticking to hands. Place dough 2 inches apart on greased baking sheet. Bake until light brown on bottoms, approximately 10 to 12 minutes. Place on wire racks to cool completely. Store in airtight container. Makes approximately 6 dozen.

Betty Lynn

LEMON BUTTER COOKIES

1 c. butter, softened (no substitute)
2 eggs, beaten
2 tsp. lemon extract
4½ c. all-purpose flour
¼ tsp. baking soda

2 c. sugar
¼ c. milk
½ tsp. salt
2 tsp. baking powder
Colored sugar (opt.)

In a mixing bowl, cream butter and sugar. Add eggs, milk and extract. Combine dry ingredients and gradually add to creamed mixture. Cover and chill for 2 hours. Roll out on lightly floured surface to ⅓-inch thickness. Cut with a 2-inch cookie cutter dipped in flour. Place 2 inches apart on ungreased baking sheets. Sprinkle with colored sugar if desired. Bake at 350° for 8 to 9 minutes or until the edges just begin to brown. Remove to wire racks to cool. Makes about 13 dozen.

Erma Donaldson

LEMON-GLAZED PERSIMMON BARS

1 c. fresh persimmon pulp (with 1½
  tsp. lemon juice or 1 c. thawed
  frozen persimmon pulp)
1 tsp. soda
½ to ¾ c. sugar
8 oz. pitted dates, finely chopped
½ tsp. salt

½ tsp. nutmeg
1 egg
½ c. salad oil
1¾ c. white flour
½ tsp. cinnamon
¼ tsp. ground cloves

Mix together and spread batter evenly in a greased and floured jellyroll pan (10 x 15 inches). Bake at 350° until lightly browned, about 25 minutes. Cool in pan for 5 minutes. Spread or dribble on glaze of your choice. Cool thoroughly and cut into bars. Makes 30 bars.

Alvina Sue

28

MACADAMIA NUT COOKIES
(Mantecaditos)

1 c. unsalted macadamia nuts
½ c. unsalted butter, softened
1 T. light rum
1⅓ c. all-purpose flour

6 T. sugar
½ tsp. salt
1 tsp. vanilla extract
Confectioners' sugar

Heat oven to 350°. Spread nuts on baking dish and bake until golden and fragrant, 5 to 7 minutes. Let stand to cool. Transfer nuts to food processor and chop to a fine powder. Cream butter until light and fluffy. Beat in sugar, salt, rum and vanilla. Stir in flour and nuts until dough holds together. (Add more flour if needed.) Form dough into 2 flat disks and cover with plastic wrap. Refrigerate at least 30 minutes. On a well-floured board, roll one disk into a circle about ³/₁₆ inch thick. Cut out circles or shape with 1½ to 2-inch cookie cutters. Transfer to cookie sheet with a thin spatula and repeat with the remaining dough. Bake until lightly brown around edges, 15 to 20 minutes. Do not overbake. Cool. Dust with powdered sugar, sifted. Ready to serve.

Lisa Lewis

OATMEAL-COCONUT COOKIES

¾ c. shortening
½ c. brown sugar
2 c. flour, sifted
1 tsp. baking powder
1 tsp. vanilla
1 c. coconut

¾ c. white sugar
1 egg
1 tsp. soda
½ tsp. salt
1 c. oatmeal
½ c. walnuts (or more)

Mix together shortening and sugars. Add egg and mix. Add flour, soda, baking powder and salt and mix. Add vanilla, oatmeal, coconut and nuts. Bake by teaspoonful on cookie sheet at 350° for 10 to 12 minutes.

Joyce O'Neal

OATMEAL DROPS

1 c. sugar
2 eggs
½ tsp. soda
5 T. milk
1 c. butter

2 c. flour
2 c. oats
½ tsp. salt
1 tsp. cinnamon
1 c. nuts

Mix all ingredients together. Drop on cookie sheet. Bake in moderate oven (350°) for 15 to 18 minutes.

Millie Baird
From Her 1940 File

ORANGE DREAM BARS

First Mixture:

½ c. margarine
½ c. brown sugar

1 c. sifted flour

Mix well and pat very thin into shallow pan. Bake at 350° for 15 minutes.

Second Mixture:

2 eggs
1 c. brown sugar
1 tsp. vanilla
½ tsp. baking powder

½ tsp. salt
1½ c. coconut
1 c. nuts

Beat eggs, sugar and vanilla. Add dry ingredients, coconut and nuts. Pour over top of baked mixture. Bake for 20 minutes. When slightly cool, add third mixture.

Third Mixture:

¾ c. powdered sugar
2 T. butter

Grated rind of 1 orange - orange juice

Cream sugar and butter. Add rind and enough juice to moisten. Frost cookies. Cut into squares.

Mildred Walters

PEANUT BUTTER SANDWICH COOKIES

1 c. butter-flavored shortening
1 c. creamy peanut butter
1 c. packed brown sugar
3 c. all-purpose flour
¼ tsp. salt

1 c. sugar
3 eggs
1 tsp. vanilla extract
2 tsp. baking soda

Filling:

½ c. creamy peanut butter
3 c. confectioners' sugar

1 tsp. vanilla extract
5 to 6 T. milk

In a mixing bowl, cream the shortening, peanut butter and sugars. Add vanilla. Add eggs, one at a time, beating well after each addition. Combine flour, baking soda and salt. Add to creamed mixture. Shape into 1-inch balls and place 2 inches apart on ungreased baking sheets. Flatten to ¾-inch thickness with a fork. Bake at 375° for 7 to 8 minutes or until golden. Cool on wire racks. In a mixing bowl, beat filling ingredients until smooth. Spread on half of the cookies and top each with another cookie. Makes about 4 dozen.

Erma Donaldson

23304-98

PEANUT BRITTLE COOKIES

Sift together:

½ **tsp. baking soda**
1 **c. flour**

½ **tsp. cinnamon**

Cream together:

½ **c. butter**
½ **c. brown sugar**

1 **tsp. vanilla**

Cream this together until light and fluffy. Blend in:

**2 T. well-beaten egg (reserve
remaining egg)**

Add 1 cup finely chopped peanuts to dry ingredients mix. Then add to creamed mixture. Spread and pat dough onto a greased 10 x 14-inch baking sheet. It will be a thin layer. Brush with remaining beaten egg. Sprinkle with ½ cup salted Spanish peanuts. (Be sure to use only the small red Spanish peanuts in this recipe. I like Planter's.) Press them into the dough a little so they will stick on it. Bake in a slow oven (325°) for 20 minutes. Do not overbake. Break into irregular-shaped pieces while warm so the pieces look like peanut brittle. Makes about 2 dozen. This recipe dates back to 1949. It is a very interesting shape and taste on a cookie tray.

Carolyn Walter

PECAN PIE BARS

1 **(18½-oz.) pkg. yellow cake mix,**
⅔ **c. reserved for filling**

½ **stick melted margarine**
1 **egg**

Combine cake mix (except for ⅔ cup) with margarine and egg. Mix until crumbly. Generously grease bottom and sides of 13 x 9-inch pan. Press in pan. Bake at 350° for 15 to 20 minutes or until golden.

Filling:

⅔ **c. cake mix**
1½ **c. corn syrup**
3 **eggs**

½ **c. brown sugar**
1 **tsp. vanilla**
1 **c. chopped pecans**

In a large bowl, combine cake mix, brown sugar, corn syrup, vanilla and eggs. Beat medium speed for 2 minutes. Pour filling over baked crust. Sprinkle chopped pecans over top. Return to 350° oven for 30 to 35 minutes, until filling is set. Cool. Cut into bars. Makes about 3 dozen and freezes well.

Mildred Walters

PERSIMMON COOKIES

4 c. persimmon pulp	4 tsp. soda
4 cubes butter	4 c. sugar
4 eggs	8 c. flour
2 tsp. cinnamon	2 tsp. cloves
2 tsp. nutmeg	4 c. nuts
4 c. raisins	

Dissolve the soda in the persimmon pulp. Cream together the butter and sugar. Add the eggs to the pulp. Mix together the flour and spices. Add nuts and raisins to flour and spices. Mix all ingredients together. Drop on cookie sheet(s). Bake for 15 to 20 minutes in moderate oven (350°).

Betty Baird

PERSIMMON COOKIES

1 tsp. soda	1 c. persimmon pulp
2 c. flour	½ tsp. cloves
½ tsp. nutmeg	½ tsp. cinnamon
½ c. margarine	1 c. sugar
1 egg	1 c. nuts, chopped
1 c. dates, chopped	1 c. raisins (opt.)

Mix soda with persimmon pulp. Sift flour and spices together. Cream margarine with sugar. Add egg. Mix pulp, flour and egg mixtures alternately. Add nuts, dates and raisins (optional). Bake at 375° for 10 to 15 minutes. A double batch makes approximately 100 to 125 cookies depending on size. These **freeze** perfectly in airtight containers.

Mildred Walters

PERSIMMON-NUT COOKIES

2 c. pulp	2 tsp. soda
2 c. sugar	1 c. butter
2 eggs	1 tsp. cloves
1 tsp. nutmeg	1 tsp. cinnamon
4 c. flour	2 c. walnuts, chopped

Mix pulp and soda and let stand. Cream together sugar, butter and eggs. Mix spices with flour. Add flour mixture to creamed mixture and mix. Add pulp mixture and walnuts. Bake on greased sheet at 350° for 20 minutes. Makes 6 dozen.

Susan Fiske

PINE NUT MACAROONS

2 lg. egg whites	⅓ c. sugar
1 T. instant coffee	1 tsp. vanilla
1 c. pine nuts or sliced almonds	

Beat egg whites until soft peaks form. Add sugar, 1 tablespoonful at a time, and beat about 30 seconds after each addition. Add coffee and vanilla. Beat until coffee

(continued)

23304-98

is completely dissolved. Gently fold in nuts. Drop by tablespoon onto greased and floured baking sheets. Bake at 325° for about 20 minutes, until golden. (Switch pan positions after 10 minutes.) Let macaroons cool 5 minutes on each sheet, then transfer to racks to cool. 40 calories each.

Joan Pharis

POTATO CHIP COOKIES

1 c. margarine
1 tsp. vanilla
½ c. crushed potato chips

½ c. sugar
½ c. chopped nuts
2 c. flour

Cream together margarine and sugar. Add vanilla, potato chips, nuts and flour. Mix well. Form into small balls and place on ungreased baking sheet. Dip small glass in sugar and flatten cookies. Bake at 350° for 16 to 18 minutes. Serves 60.

Joan Pharis

PUMPKIN PIE SQUARES

1 (13-oz.) can evaporated milk
2 tsp. pumpkin pie spice
1 c. sugar
1 lg. (1-lb. 13-oz.) can pumpkin
¾ c. butter or margarine

3 eggs, beaten
½ tsp. salt
½ c. chopped nuts
1 pkg. yellow cake mix

Combine milk, eggs, spice, salt, sugar and pumpkin. Pour into 9 x 13-inch pan. Sprinkle dry cake mix over top. Slice butter over top of cake mix. Sprinkle with nuts. Bake at 350° about 50 minutes.

Mildred Walters

RANGER COOKIES

1 c. shortening
1 c. brown sugar
1 c. white sugar
2 eggs
1 tsp. vanilla
2 c. flour

1 tsp. salt
2 c. rolled oats
2 c. cornflakes
1 c. coconut
1 tsp. baking powder
1 tsp. soda

Cream shortening and sugar. Add eggs and vanilla; mix until smooth. Add flour which has been sifted with soda, baking powder and salt. Mix thoroughly. Add oats, cornflakes and coconut. Drop by half teaspoon on greased baking sheet. After 10 minutes of baking time at 350°, brush cookies with icing made of powdered sugar and water. Bake 5 minutes longer.

Judy Burtoft

ROLLED OAT COOKIES

1 c. butter or margarine
1 c. packed brown sugar
3 c. quick oats
1¼ c. all-purpose flour

¼ c. water
1 tsp. vanilla extract
1 tsp. salt
¼ tsp. baking soda

(continued)

In a mixing bowl, cream butter and sugar. Add water and vanilla and mix well. Combine dry ingredients. Add to creamed mixture and mix well; chill for 30 minutes. Shape into 2 (1½-inch) rolls. Wrap tightly in waxed paper. Chill for 2 hours or until firm. Cut into ½-inch slices and place 2 inches apart on greased baking sheets. Bake at 375° for 12 minutes or until lightly browned. Remove to wire racks to cool. Makes about 3½ dozen.

Erma Donaldson

SHORT CUT COOKIES

Combine:

Any cake mix   **2 eggs**
⅓ c. vegetable oil

Bake as you would cookies in general at 350° for 10 to 12 minutes on cookie sheets.

Susan Fiske

BROWN SUGAR-WALNUT BARS

1 egg   **¼ tsp. salt**
1 c. brown sugar   **¼ tsp. soda**
2 tsp. vanilla   **1 c. chopped walnuts**
½ c. flour

Beat egg, brown sugar and vanilla together with electric beater until light and foamy. Add flour, salt and soda. Stir in nuts. Bake 18 to 20 minutes in greased 8-inch square pan at 350°. Cool in pan before cutting into bars. **Do not overbake.** Best when correct baking time is used. I've enjoyed this recipe since 1948.

Carolyn Walter

SIGNA'S SNOWFLAKE COOKIES

1 lb. sweet butter, softened   **1 c. white sugar**
3 c. flour   **1 tsp. vanilla**
1½ c. crushed potato chips   **Powdered sugar**

Cream butter and sugar. Add flour and vanilla; mix well. Add crushed potato chips. Drop by spoonful onto ungreased cookie sheet. Press flat but not thin. Bake at 350° for 10 to 16 minutes or until golden brown. Sprinkle powdered sugar on top. Cool. Place in freezer in covered container. Serve directly from freezer. This is very rich and delicious. Let people guess what's inside.

Pearledna Shropshire

SLEEP COOKIES

2 egg whites   **¼ to ½ tsp. vanilla**
1 c. chocolate morsels   **Pinch salt**
¼ tsp. cream of tartar   **1 c. pecans, chopped**
⅔ c. sugar

(continued)

Preheat oven to 350°. Beat egg whites until foamy. Add salt and cream of tartar and beat until stiff. Add sugar, 2 tablespoons at a time, and beat well after each addition. Fold in vanilla, chocolate and nuts. Drop by teaspoon on a sheet lined with foil. Put in oven **and turn the oven off immediately. Do not open door for at least 2 hours.** Carefully remove cookies from foil. Makes about 48 small cookies.

Mildred Walters

SNICKERDOODLES

1 c. shortening (part butter)
1½ c. sugar
2 eggs
2¾ c. flour
2 tsp. cinnamon

2 tsp. cream of tartar
1 tsp. soda
¼ tsp. salt
2 tsp. sugar

Heat oven to 400°. Mix shortening, sugar and eggs thoroughly. Measure flour and blend with soda, cream of tartar and salt. Blend shortening to mixture. Form into 1-inch balls. Roll in mixture of sugar and cinnamon. Place about 2 inches apart on ungreased baking sheet. Bake 8 to 10 minutes at 400°. Makes about 6 dozen cookies.

Barbara Lockridge

SPICE COOKIES WITH PUMPKIN DIP

1½ c. butter or margarine, softened
2 eggs
4 c. all-purpose flour
2 tsp. ground cinnamon
1 tsp. cloves
2 c. sugar

½ c. molasses
4 tsp. baking soda
1 tsp. ground ginger
1 tsp. salt
Additional sugar

Pumpkin Dip:

1 (8-oz.) pkg. cream cheese, softened
1 (18-oz.) can pumpkin pie mix

2 c. confectioners' sugar
½ to 1 tsp. ground cinnamon
¼ to ½ tsp. ground ginger

In a mixing bowl, cream butter and sugar. Add eggs, one at a time, beating well after each addition. Add molasses and mix well. Combine flour, baking soda, cinnamon, ginger, cloves and salt. Add to creamed mixture and mix well. Chill overnight. Shape into ½-inch balls and roll in sugar. Place 2 inches apart on ungreased baking sheets. Bake at 375° for 6 minutes or until edges begin to brown. Cool for 2 minutes before removing to a wire rack. **Dip:** Beat cream cheese in a mixing bowl until smooth. Add pumpkin pie mix and beat well. Add sugar, cinnamon and ginger and beat until smooth. Serve with cookies. Store leftover dip in the refrigerator. Yields about 20 dozen (3 cups dip).

Erma Donaldson

STRAWBERRY DELIGHT COOKIES

1 c. (2 sticks) unsalted butter, softened
1 dab strawberry jam
1 (3-oz.) pkg. cream cheese, softened

2 c. all-purpose flour
½ c. sugar
1 tsp. vanilla extract

Preheat oven to 350°. Mix butter and cream cheese. Beat in sugar and vanilla. Stir in flour until well mixed. Use ½ tablespoon to measure mixture, then shape into small balls and place 2 inches apart on ungreased cookie sheet. Make small indentation with your thumb. Carefully place strawberry jam in center of each cookie. Bake for 12 to 18 minutes or until lightly browned. Cool on racks. Makes 5 dozen.

Marguerite McClure

SUGAR COOKIES

1½ lbs. butter
4½ c. sugar
1½ tsp. cream of tartar
1½ tsp. vanilla

9 c. flour
1 T. baking soda
5 eggs
1½ tsp. salt

Mix all ingredients well. Roll thin; cut and bake at 350° for 10 to 12 minutes. Decorate with powdered sugar icing and colored sugar sprinkles.

Charlotte White

TEATIME TASSIES

1 (3-oz.) pkg. cream cheese
½ c. butter

1 c. flour, sifted

Let cream cheese and butter soften to room temperature. Blend together. Stir in flour. Chill for 1 hour. Shape into 20 small balls. Press each one into small Swedish tart pans for crust.

Nut Filling:

1 egg
1 T. butter, softened
¾ c. brown sugar

1 T. vanilla
Nuts

Beat egg, brown sugar, butter and vanilla until smooth. Put half the nuts in the 20 tart pans. Add egg mixture and top with rest of the nuts. Bake at 325° for 25 minutes. Cool and remove from pans.

Mildred Walters

UNBAKED CHOCOLATE COOKIES

3 c. quick oats
1 (6-oz.) pkg. chocolate chips
1 c. coconut

1 c. chopped walnuts
1 c. raisins

Mix these ingredients into a large bowl.

(continued)

23304-98

1 c. brown sugar
½ c. milk
Pinch salt

1 c. white sugar
¼ lb. margarine

Put into a saucepan and bring to a boil. Stir boiled mixture into the dry ingredients in large bowl until chocolate is melted and all is well mixed. Drop by teaspoon onto waxed paper.

Elaine Straube

UNCOCONUT COOKIES

1 cube margarine
1½ c. Bisquick
1 tsp. coconut flavoring

1½ c. Betty Crocker Potato Buds
1 egg
1 c. sugar

Mix all ingredients well. Drop by teaspoon on lightly greased pan or cookie sheet. Bake 12 minutes at 350°.

Marge Todd

WORLD'S BEST COOKIES

1 c. butter (2 cubes)
1 c. brown sugar, well packed
1 c. vegetable oil
1 c. oatmeal, uncooked
1 c. crushed cornflakes
½ c. shredded coconut
½ c. chopped pecans (2 oz.)

3½ c. all-purpose flour
1 c. granulated sugar
1 egg
1 tsp. vanilla
1 tsp. baking soda
1 tsp. salt

Cream butter and sugar until light and fluffy. Add egg and mix well. Add oatmeal, cornflakes, coconut, pecans and vanilla; stir well. Add flour, baking soda and salt and mix. Form into 1-inch balls. Place on an ungreased baking sheet. Flatten with a fork dipped in water. Bake at 350° for 10 minutes. Cool on baking sheet 10 minutes before removing. Makes about 9½ dozen.

Jean Edwards

SPRITZ COOKIES

1 c. shortening (½ butter)
1 egg
2¼ c. flour, sifted
¼ tsp. baking powder

¾ c. sugar
1 tsp. vanilla
½ tsp. salt

Cream shortening and sugar well. Beat in egg and vanilla. Gradually blend in dry ingredients which have been sifted together. Fill cookie press and form cookies on ungreased cookie sheets. Bake at 375° for 10 to 12 minutes. You may decorate these or serve them plain. Makes about 5 dozen.

Linda Dungan

ALMOND TOFFEE

1 c. butter (not margarine)
1 c. chopped almonds (set aside ¼ c.)

1¼ c. sugar
1 (6-oz.) pkg. chocolate chips

Melt butter over low heat in a 3-quart saucepan. Add sugar and ¾ cup of the almonds. Turn heat to high and stir rapidly until color changes to a light caramel, about 5 minutes. **Do not overcook.** Remove from heat and pour at once into a slightly warmed ungreased 13 x 9 x 2-inch pan. Spread as thin as possible. Pour chocolate chips on top and spread evenly with a knife as they melt. Sprinkle the remaining ¼ cup of almonds on top. Let harden for 3 hours. Break into pieces. Store in refrigerator until serving time. This is an easy no-fail recipe!

Joanne Carter

ANITA ESTRADA'S EASY CANDY

12 oz. butterscotch chips
1 c. cocktail peanuts

2 c. canned Chinese noodles

Melt morsels in double boiler. Add the rest; stir. Drop on waxed paper. Cool. Can be frozen. Anita is from family of old Estradas restaurant in Visalia.

Betty Baird

CANDIED CITRUS PEEL

Using scissors cut citrus peel in strips. Place pan of sugar syrup on low back burner (a cup of sugar to each 2 cups water). Put snipped peel in kettle. Then do this process 3 times; cover with cold water. Bring to boil; boil 8 minutes. Drain. Cover the peel with the sugar syrup plus more water and sugar if needed to cover peel. Boil for about 20 minutes. Let soak in syrup a few hours, then drain several hours. Turn out onto a cookie sheet. Dry out enough so sugar won't turn to syrup, but not enough to be hard. A dehydrator would be great. Sunshine might work. I've tried a slow oven. When dry enough to hold sugar, place in covered container in refrigerator. Resugar and shake every day for a while as needed. I put a crumpled paper towel, dry or moist as needed, in container.

Phyllis Morgan
Habitat for Humanity

CANDIED GRAPEFRUIT

2 grapefruit, cut in bite-sized pieces
(be sure to remove seeds)

Cover with cold water and cook for 30 minutes. Do this 3 times, pouring off water and covering with fresh cold water each time. Drain. Add 4½ cups of sugar and add almost 1 cup of water. Cook for **hours**, slowly, until all cooks down, stirring often. Take out of pan and lay on waxed paper. Let stand overnight. Roll in sugar the next day.

Elaine Straube

23304-98

MARZIPAN CHOCOLATE KISSES

3¼-oz. pkg. slivered almonds
½ c. powdered sugar
1 T. + 2 tsp. light corn syrup
1 tsp. almond extract
¼ tsp. red food coloring
5-oz. pkg. (24) milk chocolate
 Kisses, unwrapped
Granulated sugar

Put slivered almonds in blender; cover and blend at high speed until very finely chopped. Pour into mixing bowl and combine with powdered sugar. Combine corn syrup, almond extract and food coloring. Drizzle into almond mixture. Stir until slightly blended. Mix with hands until mixture clings together. Press about 1 teaspoon mixture around a Kiss, maintaining the Kiss shape. Roll in granulated sugar. Store in airtight container. Makes about 24.

Variations: Instead of almond extract and red food coloring, substitute the following: **Orange:** ¾ teaspoon orange extract, 7 drops red and 14 drops orange food coloring. **Lemon:** ¾ teaspoon lemon extract and ¼ teaspoon yellow food coloring. **Green:** ¾ teaspoon peppermint extract and ¼ teaspoon green food coloring. When done, these will resemble miniature snow-covered Christmas trees.

Marge Lowery

SEE'S CHOCOLATE FUDGE

3 sm. pkgs. chocolate chips or 1½
 lg. pkgs.
2 to 4 c. walnuts, broken
2 cubes butter or margarine
1 (7-oz.) jar marshmallow creme
2 T. vanilla

Put top ingredients in a large mixing bowl. Butter 2 (9 x 13-inch) pans to pour candy in. In a large heavy saucepan put:

4½ c. sugar   1 lg. can Borden's milk

Mix with wooden spoon and stir constantly over medium heat, bringing to a rolling boil; boil 6 minutes. Pour over other ingredients and stir until mixture begins to set up. Pour into buttered pan. Spread and let cool. Set in a cool place. (I often leave it overnight before cutting.) Makes 5 pounds.

Gladys Bessey

SWEET NOTHINGS

1 cube butter or margarine
½ c. peanut butter
6 oz. chocolate chips

Melt in microwave 3 minutes on medium. Add 6 cups Rice Chex and mix well. Put 2 cups powdered sugar in paper bag. Add Rice Chex and shake until all are covered with sugar. Cool on cookie sheet.

Joan Pharis

ALMOND ROCA

1 c. butter
1 c. sugar
½ c. finely chopped almonds
4 oz. milk chocolate bar

(continued)

Cook butter and sugar to hard candy stage, 300°-310°, on a real low fire, stirring constantly. Take up and add ½ of nuts. Spread on buttered pan. Spread on melted chocolate and rest of nuts. Cool.

Joyce O'Neal

Recipe Favorites

23304-98

Pies,
Pastry
&
Desserts

Helpful Hints

• Vinegar can remove spots caused by tomatoes. Soak spot with vinegar and wash as usual.

• To freshen your dishwasher, run it on rinse with some baking soda.

• Drops of oil of cinnamon, cotton balls soaked in your favorite perfume or disinfectant will leave room smelling fresh after you vacuum.

• Things to keep in the kitchen: a ruler, scissors, small hammer, flashlight, candles, matches and tape.

• Egg whites need to be room temperature for greater volume when whipped.

• To freeze eggs: Spray ice cube trays with oil. Beat eggs and add 3/4 teaspoon sugar and 1/4 teaspoon salt for every 1/2 dozen. Pour into trays and freeze firm. Store in airtight containers in freezer. One cube equals one egg.

• A leaf of lettuce dropped into the pot absorbs the grease from the top of the soup. Remove the lettuce and throw it away as soon as it has served its purpose.

• Use steel wool covered with fabric for a pin and needle sharpener. Attach curtain rings on drawstring ties and the ties will not come out.

• Separate 2 glasses by filling the inside one with cold water and setting the other in hot.

• Old Amish Proverb: Eat it up, wear it out, make it do, or do without!

• Organize coloring books and crayons with a dish drainer.

• For quick and handy seasoning while cooking, keep on hand a large shaker containing six parts of salt and one of pepper.

• Before scalding milk, rinse pan with cold water for easy clean up.

• Getting the catsup out of the bottle isn't so tough. Insert a drinking straw, push it to the bottom of the bottle, and then remove. Enough air will be admitted to start an even flow.

• Add a lump of butter or a few teaspoons of cooking oil to the water. Rice, noodles or spaghetti will not boil over or stick together.

PIES, PASTRY & DESSERTS

AUNT MARY'S BURNT SUGAR PIE

In a saucepan, brown:

½ **c. sugar**

Add:

½ **c. water**

Cook until dissolved. Add:

½ **c. sugar**   **3 eggs**
⅓ **c. flour**   **3 T. butter**
1½ **c. milk**

Cook until thickened and top with a meringue.

Joan Pharis

FALL PEAR PIE

8 c. thinly sliced, peeled pears   **1 egg, lightly beaten**
¼ **c. quick-cooking tapioca**   ¼ **c. heavy cream (opt.)**
¼ **tsp. ground nutmeg**   **1 (9-inch) pastry for double-crust**
¾ **c. sugar**   **pie**

In a large bowl, combine pears, sugar, tapioca and nutmeg. Line a pie plate with bottom crust. Add pear mixture. Roll out remaining pastry to fit top of pie. Cut large slits in top. Place over filling; seal and flute edges. Brush with egg. Bake at 375° for 55 to 60 minutes or until the pears are tender. Remove to a wire rack. Pour cream through slits if desired.

Erma Donaldson

ROYAL PEAR PIE

Prepare pastry for 2-crust 9-inch pie.

6 med. pears, peeled, cored &   **1 tsp. cinnamon**
    sliced   1½ **T. cornstarch**
1 T. lemon juice   **Dash salt**
Grated rind from ½ **lemon**   **1 T. margarine**
¾ **c. brown or white sugar**

Combine all ingredients except margarine. Pour into pie shell. Dot with margarine. Cover with top crust. Make 2 slits or prick well. Bake at 425° for 45 minutes or until done.

Marge Lowery

STRAWBERRY PIE

1 pt. vanilla ice cream
1 (3½ oz.) strawberry Jello
1½ c. water

1 c. sliced strawberries, cut in
fourths

Dissolve Jello in 1 cup hot water. Stir in ½ cup cold water. Add pint of vanilla ice cream. Stir until melted. Chill until thickened. Garnish with whipped cream and sliced strawberries.

Mary Morey

STRAWBERRY PIE

1 deep-dish 9-inch pastry, cooked
3 baskets nice, clean strawberries

1 jar strawberry glaze, poured over

Chill 1 hour. Top with whipped cream. Garnish with beautiful sliced strawberries and mint leaves.

Mary Morey

SUGAR-FREE APPLE PIE

4 or 5 c. peeled Golden Delicious
  apples
⅔ c. frozen apple juice
  concentrate, undiluted
2 tsp. tapioca

½ tsp. lemon juice
½ tsp. cinnamon (or less if desired)
A few shakes ground nutmeg or
  freshly grated nutmeg

Divide your favorite pastry in two parts. Line pie plate and set aside. Mix apple juice, tapioca, cinnamon, nutmeg and lemon juice. Stir apples and liquid together. Put a piece of apple into mixture to check desired spices. Pour apples in pie shell. Roll top and cover pie. Brush top with milk and sprinkle with a pinch of sugar. Cut desired design in top. Cover edge with foil. Bake at 425° for 15 minutes, then remove foil from edge and lower heat to 350° and bake for 45 minutes more or until apples are bubbly and done.

Carolyn Walter

APPLE DUMPLINGS

2 c. sugar
2 c. water
¼ tsp. cinnamon
¼ c. butter
8 apples

2 c. flour
1 tsp. salt
2 tsp. baking powder
¾ c. shortening
½ c. milk

Peel and core apples. Sift flour, salt and baking powder. Cut in shortening. Add milk and stir until moist. Roll out ¼ inch thick. Cut into 5-inch squares. Place apples on squares. Sprinkle with sugar and cinnamon. Dot with butter. Fold corners. Place 1 inch apart on greased baking pan. Pour over sauce. Bake at 375° for 35 minutes. **Sauce:** Combine sugar, water and cinnamon. Cook 5 minutes. Serve hot with cream!

Judy Burtoft

23304-98

APPLE GOODY

Part A:

1 c. sugar
⅛ c. flour
Pinch salt

1⅛ tsp. cinnamon
2 to 2½ cans chopped apples

Part B:

1½ c. dry oatmeal
1 c. brown sugar
¾ c. flour

⅜ tsp. baking powder
⅜ tsp. soda
⅞ c. butter

Mix sugar, flour, salt and cinnamon in Part A. Add apples and mix. Put into greased baking pan. Mix oatmeal, sugar, flour, baking powder and soda (Part B). Add butter and work with fingertips until mixture is crumbly. Place mixture over apples and pat firmly. Bake at 350° until crust is formed and apples are tender. Serve hot or cold with milk or cream.

Judy Burtoft

CHERRY SUPREME

2 cans cherry pie filling
1½ cubes butter

1 pkg. yellow cake mix
About 1 c. walnuts

Mix together ½ of butter (melted) and ½ of cake mix with about ¾ cup of the chopped nuts. Press in bottom of pan. Add cherries and the remaining cake mix. Pour remainder of melted butter over top. Sprinkle with walnuts. Bake at 350° for 45 minutes.

Ruth Caudill

CHERRY SUPREME

2 cans cherry pie filling
1 pkg. dry yellow cake mix
1 cube butter, melted

1 pkg. slivered almonds (can be substituted)

Spray 9 x 13-inch pan with Pam. Spread 2 cans cherry pie filling on bottom of pan. Spread one package dry yellow cake mix over cherries. Melt 1 cube butter and spread over cake mix. Spread 1 package slivered almonds (or any nuts available) over top. Bake at 350° for 1 hour.

Alice Anderson

CHOCOLATE DESSERT

1 c. all-purpose flour
½ tsp. salt
2 T. ground chocolate
½ c. chopped nuts
2 T. shortening, melted

1 tsp. vanilla
2 tsp. baking powder
⅔ c. sugar
½ c. milk

(continued)

Sift dry ingredients together and add milk, chopped nuts, melted shortening and vanilla. Stir well and pour into greased pan about 6 x 10 inches.

Topping:

¼ **c. white sugar**
3 **T. ground chocolate**

½ **c. brown sugar**
¼ **tsp. salt**

Mix the above ingredients and shake out on top of cake. Pour 1 cup boiling water on top of all. Place in 350° oven and bake 45 minutes. Serves 8.

Mildred Walters

CHOCOLATE RICH CRESCENT CROISSANT

8 **oz. Pillsbury refrigerated quick**
crescent dinner rolls
2 **T. margarine or butter, softened**
(opt.)
4-**oz. bar sweet baking chocolate**

1 **egg, beaten with fork**
2 **T. sliced or slivered almonds or**
walnuts
Powdered sugar

Heat oven to 375°. Separate dough into 8 triangles. Press each triangle to slightly enlarge; spread with margarine. Break or cut chocolate bar into small pieces (chocolate may break into irregular shapes). Place an equal amount of chocolate pieces on shortest side of each triangle. Roll up, starting at shortest side of each triangle and rolling to opposite point. Place rolls, point side down, on ungreased cookie sheet. Curve into crescent shape. Brush rolls with beaten egg; sprinkle with nuts. Bake at 375° for 11 to 13 minutes or until golden brown. Cool. Sprinkle with powdered sugar.

Ruth Wills

FINGER JELLO

You may want to grease a pan with a little mayonnaise. This is good for the convalescing child.

4 **boxes unflavored gelatin mixed**
with 3 boxes Jello

4 **c. boiling water**

Add water to Jello. Pour in flat pan; chill. Cut into cubes or strips for finger eating.

Betty Baird

23304-98

FRUIT & NUT RING

⅔ c. chopped pecans or walnuts
½ c. finely chopped dates
¼ c. raisins or currants (opt.)
1 T. sugar
⅛ tsp. cinnamon
8-oz. can Pillsbury refrigerated
quick crescent dinner rolls

¼ c. apricot preserves, warmed
slightly in microwave to soften
1 egg white, slightly beaten with
fork (or whole egg)
1 T. water
Sugar to sprinkle on top

Glaze:

½ c. powdered sugar
2 to 3 tsp. milk

¼ tsp. vanilla

Heat oven to 350°. In a small bowl, combine nuts, dates, raisins, 1 tablespoon sugar and cinnamon. Unroll dough into 2 long rectangles. Overlap edges and perforations to seal. Press to form 16 x 7-inch rectangle. Spread preserves over dough to within 1 inch of edges; sprinkle with nut mixture, starting with sugar. Bake at 350° for 24 to 30 minutes or until golden brown. In small bowl combine glaze ingredients; drizzle over warm ring.

Ruth Wills

FRUIT PIZZA

Crust:

½ c. margarine
½ c. sugar
1 egg
1 tsp. cream of tartar

1 tsp. vanilla
2½ c. flour
¼ c. oil
¼ tsp. salt

Mix all ingredients. Spread and press onto 2 (12-inch) greased pizza pans or 1 large greased cookie sheet. Bake at 350° for 10 to 15 minutes; cool.

Filling:

16 oz. cream cheese
½ c. sugar

2 tsp. vanilla

Mix and spread on cooled crust.

Topping:

Fresh fruit placed over filling

You may use canned fruits (kiwi, cherries, peaches, strawberries, blueberries, guava, etc.).

Glaze:

1 c. orange juice
¾ c. water
Dash salt

¾ c. sugar
¼ c. cornstarch

(continued)

Mix and cook over medium heat until thick, stirring constantly. Pour over fruit. Chill and serve.

Joyce O'Neal

PERSIMMON PUDDING

1 c. flour
1 tsp. soda
½ tsp. salt
1 tsp. cinnamon
1 egg, beaten
1 c. raisins
1 tsp. vanilla

1 c. sugar
1 tsp. baking powder
2 tsp. butter
1 c. persimmon pulp
¼ c. milk
1 c. chopped nuts

Mix together. Place in covered baking dish. Put baking dish in a pan of water. Bake at 350° for 1½ hours.

Ruth Caudill

PHARIS' FAVORITE APPLE CRISP

4 c. sliced apples
½ tsp. salt
¾ c. flour
⅓ c. butter

1 tsp. cinnamon
¼ c. water
1 c. sugar

Place in buttered dish: sliced apples sprinkled with sugar, salt and water. Rub together: flour, sugar and butter. Drop this mixture over apples. Bake at 350° for about 40 minutes.

Joan Pharis

PUMPKIN CRUNCH

1 lg. (29-oz.) can pumpkin
1 c. evaporated milk
2 tsp. pumpkin pie spice
1 pkg. spice cake mix (or yellow cake mix)

3 eggs
1 c. sugar
1 cube butter
Nuts

Mix pumpkin, sugar, milk, eggs and spice. Pour into greased 9 x 13-inch pan. Cut the butter into cake mix until crumbly. Spoon over mixture in pan. Serves 12 to 15 generously.

Marge Todd

Main
Dishes
&
Casseroles

Helpful Hints

• When preparing a casserole, make additional batches to freeze. Then, when there isn't time to plan a meal or when unexpected guests appear, simply take the casserole from the freezer and pop it in the oven.

• To keep hot oil from splattering, sprinkle a little salt or flour in the pan before frying.

• Never overcook foods that are to be frozen. Foods will finish cooking while being heated. Don't refreeze cooked thawed foods.

• Don't freeze spaghetti, macaroni or noodle mixtures. These tend to lose texture and become too soft when reheated.

• Green pepper may change the flavor in frozen casseroles. Clove, garlic and pepper flavors get stronger when they are frozen, while sage, onion, and salt get milder or fade out.

• Don't freeze cooked egg white — it becomes tough.

• Spray your grill with vegetable oil to prevent sticking.

• Instant potatoes are a good thickener for stews.

• When freezing foods, label each container with the contents and the date it was put into the freezer. Store at 0°. Always use frozen cooked foods within one to two months.

• After purchasing, store dried pasta, rice (except brown rice), and whole grains in tightly covered containers in a cool, dry place. Refrigerate brown rice. Refrigerate or freeze grains if they will not be used within five months.

• Glazed pottery, earthenware, glass, metal…take your pick. All can be used for casseroles. Many of these casserole containers come in bright colors and pleasing designs to contrast or complement your kitchen decor or tableware. The type of container you use makes very little difference, as long as it is heat-proof. Some of the earliest casseroles were made of earthenware and were glazed inside. They had covers and were similar to those that are still used today.

• Souffle dishes are especially designed to help your souffle climb to magnificent heights. A souffle dish has straight sides. Ramekins are good for serving individual casseroles.

MAIN DISHES

1-2-3 ENCHILADAS

2 c. cooked shredded chicken
3 c. Monterey Jack cheese (or low-fat cheese)
1/2 c. chopped onion
1 (19-oz.) can green chili enchilada sauce

8 corn tortillas
3/4 c. sour cream (fat-free or other)
1 (4.5-oz.) can chopped green chilies

In a small bowl, combine chicken, 2 cups cheese, chilies and onion. In small skillet, bring sauce to boil; remove from heat. Dip each tortilla into heated sauce to soften. Spoon 1/3 cup chicken mixture and 2 tablespoons sour cream down center of each tortilla. Roll tortillas and place them, seam side down, in 12 x 8-inch baking dish. Pour remaining heated sauce over top. Sprinkle with remaining cheese. Bake 20 minutes at 350°. Serves 4 to 8.

Joan Pharis

ALMOND RICE

1 lb. cooked pork shoulder, cut into 1-inch squares
1 lg. onion, diced
1/2 bell pepper, diced
1 c. celery, diced

1 c. raw rice
2 pkgs. Lipton chicken noodle soup mix
1 pkg. chopped almonds
Salt & pepper to taste

Brown meat, onion, pepper and celery in skillet. Add raw rice and brown. To 4 1/2 cups boiling water, add noodle soup mix and boil about 7 minutes. Add meat mixture and almonds. Put in covered casserole dish. Bake 1 hour at 375°.

Nancy Anderson

BEAN CASSEROLE

1 can French-style green beans
1 can whole yellow wax beans
1 can bean sprouts
1 can water chestnuts, sliced

1 can mushrooms
1 can French-fried onion rings
1 can mushroom soup

Drain liquid from everything except mushrooms. Dilute soup with mushroom liquid. Mix all vegetables together and place in casserole. Pour soup over all. Dot with butter and season with salt and pepper. Bake about 20 minutes at 325°. Remove from oven and place onion rings on top. Return to oven and bake 15 minutes longer.

Joan Pharis

BEEF LASAGNA

1 bag med. flour tortillas
1 lb. ground beef
1 med. can enchilada sauce

1 lb. shredded cheddar cheese
1 can olives, chopped
1 med. onion, chopped

(continued)

Brown beef and drain. Spray a casserole dish with Pam. Layers of tortilla, beef, olives, onion, cheese. (Make several layers. Last layer of cheese.) Bake in moderate oven for 20 to 25 minutes or until sauce and cheese have melted.

Basil Anderson

BEEF STEW FOR 25

8 lbs. boneless chuck, trimmed &
  cut for stew meat
8 lbs. potatoes, diced
2 lbs. onions, diced
2 lbs. carrots, diced

2 bunches celery, diced
1½ qt. tomatoes
2 pkgs. beef stew seasoning
Salt & pepper to taste
Flour

Dredge meat in flour. Brown in oil in a large heavy skillet. Transfer to cooker. Add all other ingredients. Cook for 3 hours.

Jean Edwards

BROCCOLI-CHICKEN DIVAN SANDWICHES

10 oz. chopped broccoli, frozen
2 c. chicken or turkey meat,
  cooked & chopped
½ c. mayonnaise

1 tsp. mustard
½ tsp. Worcestershire sauce
Dash lemon juice
Bread

Cook broccoli according to package directions. Drain well, then cool slightly. Combine with remaining ingredients except bread. Use as spread on bread. Can be broiled with grated cheese on top.

Cindi Rogers

BROILED TURKEY & APPLE SANDWICHES

2½ c. turkey light meat, skinless,
  chopped
1 apple, cored & chopped
1 c. cheddar cheese, shredded

⅔ c. mayonnaise, imitation, no
  cholesterol
6 slices bread

Combine all ingredients except bread. Toast bread slightly under broiler; turn and toast other side. Spoon turkey mixture onto slices and broil until hot and bubbly. Serve open-face at once.

Cindi Rogers

BRUNCH BAKED EGGS

2 lbs. shredded Jack cheese
1 lb. mushrooms, sliced
½ med. onion, chopped
¼ c. chopped red or green pepper
¼ c. butter or margarine
8 beaten eggs
1¾ c. milk

½ c. flour
1 T. fresh chives or green onion
2 T. basil, tarragon, thyme
  (combined)
8 oz. or more cubed or strips of
  ham

(continued)

23304-98

Sprinkle 1/2 of cheese in bottom of 9 x 13-inch pan. Sauté onion, pepper, mushrooms in butter until tender but not brown. Drain well. Place on top of cheese. Arrange ham on top of vegetables. Put remaining cheese on ham. Cover and chill overnight in refrigerator. Combine milk, eggs, flour, chives, parsley. Pour on top of cheese and vegetables that have been chilled. Bake at 350° about 45 minutes. Let stand 10 minutes before cutting.

Betty Baird

BURGER WILD RICE BAKE

1 lb. lean ground beef
3 ribs celery, sliced
1½ c. uncooked WILD RICE
  (soaked overnight before using)
1 green pepper, chopped

4 c. chicken broth
½ lb. fresh mushrooms, sliced
Oil, if needed, to sauté
1 lg. onion, chopped

Crumble the ground beef into a large skillet and sauté until the beef loses its pink color. Drain off any fat. Transfer the meat to a 3-quart shallow oblong casserole. In the same skillet, adding as little oil as is possible, sauté the celery, onion, mushrooms and green pepper just until the vegetables begin to soften slightly, about 3 minutes. Combine the sautéed vegetables with the beef, wild rice and broth in the casserole; stir well. Bake, covered, at 350° for 1½ hours, stirring once or twice during baking. Uncover during last 15 minutes of baking time to evaporate any excess liquid and brown the top. Serves 8 to 10.

Marge Todd

CELERY CASSEROLE

8 c. celery, sliced in diagonal
  pieces
2 cans celery soup
½ can slivered almonds

1 can sliced water chestnuts
½ stick melted butter
½ pkg. Pepperidge Farm herb
  stuffing

Cook celery slightly and drain. Mix all ingredients except stuffing. Put ½ stuffing in bottom of 7½ x 12-inch casserole or larger. Add other ingredients. Put the remaining ½ stuffing on top. Bake 1 hour at 300°. Serves 8 to 10.

Fran Delano

CHEESE GRITS

1 c. grits, cooked according to box
  directions
1 stick Kraft garlic cheese

1 stick margarine
2 eggs, beaten with milk to make ¾
  c.

While grits are still hot, add margarine and cheese in bits. Stir until melted. Add egg and milk mixture. Place in buttered casserole. Sprinkle a little cheese on top. Bake at 350° for 40 minutes. This is also a good side dish with baked ham dinner.

Fran Delano

CHEESEBURGER PIE

1 tube crescent rolls
½ tsp. salt
Sm. amount. onion
6-oz. can tomato paste
¼ c. butter
¼ to ½ tsp. Italian seasoning

1 c. mozzarella cheese
1 lb. hamburger
½ tsp. pepper
¾ c. water
1 tsp. brown sugar
½ c. grated cheese

Press crescent rolls in bottom of glass pie pan to make crust. Brown hamburger with salt, pepper and onion. Drain and put in pie crust. In saucepan, put tomato paste, water, butter, sugar and Italian seasoning. Boil and pour over hamburger mixture. Cover with cheeses. Bake at 350° for 25 to 30 minutes.

Linda Parley
Lutheran Church in Minnesota

CHICKEN-BROCCOLI CASSEROLE

3 chicken breasts or 1 whole
  chicken, boiled until meat comes
  off bone, cooled enough to handle
3 pkgs. broccoli spears, cooked or
  raw
2 cans cream of chicken soup

1 c. mayonnaise
2 tsp. curry powder
1 (4-oz.) pkg. grated cheddar
  cheese
2 c. buttered bread, cubed

Debone chicken and place on bottom of casserole. Add layer of broccoli. Spread on soup that has been mixed with mayonnaise and curry. Add cheese layer. Top with buttered bread cubes. Bake, covered, 1 hour at 350°. (Remove cover the last 10 minutes). **Or** microwave about 20 minutes.

Doug Baird

CHICKEN, DRESSED FOR DINNER

1 can cream of celery or cream of
  chicken soup
⅓ c. mayonnaise
2 tsp. paprika
2 whole chicken breasts, split,
  skinned & boned (1 lb. boneless)

2 c. thinly sliced vegetables
  (combination of celery, green
  pepper, sweet red pepper or green
  onion)
Hot cooked rice

Microwave: In 2-quart microwave-safe casserole, blend first 3 ingredients; stir in chicken and vegetables. Cover; microwave on **high** for 10 minutes or until chicken is no longer pink, turning chicken once during cooking. Let stand, covered, for 5 minutes. Stir before serving. Serve over rice. **Conventional:** In skillet, blend first 3 ingredients; stir in chicken and vegetables. Over medium heat, heat to boiling. Reduce heat to low. Cover; simmer 20 minutes or until chicken is tender, stirring occasionally.

Marge Todd

23304-98

CHILI RELLENO CASSEROLE

1½ lbs. Jack cheese
4 sm. cans green chiles, drained
1 can evaporated milk

4 beaten eggs
2 T. flour
½ tsp. salt

In an 11 x 14-inch Pyrex dish, layer ½ chile and ½ cheese twice. Mix other ingredients in a bowl. Pour over cheese layers. Bake at 350° for 1 hour.

Joyce O'Neal

CHILI RELLENO TORTA

½ lb. cheddar cheese, grated
½ lb. Monterey Jack cheese, grated
½ c. all-purpose flour
1⅔ c. half & half

¼ c. picante sauce
1 (4-oz.) can diced green chilies, drained
5 eggs

Preheat oven to 375°. Mix cheeses and spread evenly in buttered 10-inch pie plate. Beat eggs. Add flour slowly and then beat in half & half. If mixture is lumpy, strain it. Pour egg mixture over cheeses in plate. Carefully spoon chilies over all. Spoon picante sauce over all. Bake about 45 minutes or until center is set. Serves 8 to 10.

Marguerite McClure

CLAM SPAGHETTI

1 lg. onion, chopped
6½ oz. mushroom pieces, canned & drained
2 cans clams, canned & minced
Dash salt
1 lb. spaghetti

3 tsp. basil, dried
1 tsp. garlic powder
4 T. olive oil
Parmesan cheese
Dash pepper

Start water boiling for spaghetti noodles. Over medium-low heat, sauté onions in oil until onion is clear. Add **undrained** clams, mushrooms, basil (crush before adding), garlic powder, plus a dash of salt and pepper. Simmer at least 5 minutes over low heat. Cook spaghetti noodles in boiling water for only 7 minutes; noodles should be al dente (slightly undercooked, still chewy, but not crunchy). Drain noodles; add to simmering sauce. Serve immediately sprinkled with Parmesan cheese.

Cindi Rogers

EASY NOODLES & BROCCOLI

6 T. oil
1 pkg. broccoli, frozen, chopped
1 can chicken broth, condensed

8 oz. egg noodles
¼ tsp. garlic powder
1 soup can water

(continued)

Thaw broccoli in oil. Add noodles and garlic, stirring until coated. Add broth and water; heat to boiling. Reduce heat and simmer, covered, until noodles are tender and liquid is absorbed.

Note: Add chicken or turkey meat for a main dish.

Cindi Rogers

EGG SOUFFLÉ CASSEROLE

1½ lbs. pork sausage or turkey sausage
4 eggs, beaten (can use EggBeaters)
2½ c. milk
2½ c. shredded cheese

3 c. plain croutons
1 can cream of mushroom soup
1 (2½-oz.) jar sliced mushrooms, drained
⅔ c. milk

Cook sausage in large skillet until browned. Drain and set aside. Combine eggs, 2½ cups milk and mustard. Layer croutons, cheese, sausage and egg mixture in a buttered 13 x 9-inch baking pan. Cover and chill overnight. Combine remaining ingredients; stir well and spread over top of layered mixture. Bake, uncovered, at 300° for 1½ hours.

Joan Pharis

EGGS & CHEESE TETRAZZINI

6 lg. eggs, hard-boiled, chopped
16 oz. thin spaghetti
2 cans chicken broth, condensed
2 c. water
2 T. mustard, prepared
½ tsp. salt (opt.)

¼ c. blue cheese, crumbled
6 T. oil
6 T. flour
⅔ c. powdered milk
8 oz. cream cheese
2 tsp. onion powder

While spaghetti cooks, combine oil and flour in saucepan. Stir in broth, water and powdered milk. Cook mixture over medium heat, stirring constantly, until sauce thickens. Add cream cheese in small pieces into sauce along with mustard, onion powder and salt. Stir over low heat until cheese melts. Add blue cheese crumbles and chopped eggs. Combine sauce and cooked spaghetti. Serve immediately.

Cindi Rogers

E Z LASAGNA

1 lb. lean ground beef
¼ c. chopped onion
2 tsp. dried basil leaves
1 tsp. dried oregano leaves
3 (8-oz.) cans tomato sauce
1 lb. grated skim milk mozzarella cheese

1-pt. ctn. low-fat cottage cheese
Grated Parmesan cheese
6 wide lasagna noodles
¼ tsp. garlic powder
1 tsp. salt
½ T. sugar

Brown ground beef and chopped onion; drain. Add salt, sugar, basil leaves, oregano leaves and tomato sauce. Let simmer while you cook lasagna noodles according to package directions. Drain noodles. Spray a 2-quart baking dish with Pam. Lay

(continued)

23304-98

3 noodles on bottom of pan; spread half the cottage cheese on top of noodles. Sprinkle ½ pound mozzarella cheese next; spoon ½ the meat sauce on top of cheeses. Sprinkle Parmesan cheese liberally on top of meat sauce. Repeat the layers. Bake in 400° oven for 30 minutes. Let stand for 10 minutes before serving.

Note: I serve green salad and sliced French bread as side dishes.

Ellen Fritz Wallace

FRENCH OVEN BEEF STEW

2 lbs. beef, cut in 1½-inch pieces
2 med. onions, cut in 8ths
3 stalks celery, cut diagonally
4 med. carrots, cut in half
  crosswise, then lengthwise
1 c. tomato juice
⅓ c. quick-cooking tapioca

1 T. sugar
1 T. salt
¼ tsp. pepper
½ tsp. basil
2 med. potatoes, cut in ¼-inch
  slices

Combine all ingredients, except the potatoes, in a 2½-quart casserole. Cover and bake at 300° for 2½ hours. Mix in the potatoes and cook, uncovered, 1 hour longer. Stir occasionally. I like to serve this over pastry rounds, an idea borrowed from Marie Callender's.

Dorothy Anderson

GREEN BEAN CASSEROLE

2 cans mushroom soup OR 1 can
  celery & 1 can mushroom soup
1 lg. pkg. slivered almonds
2 c. grated cheddar cheese or Jack
  cheese

3 or 4 cans French-style green
  beans
Dried onions to taste

Combine in layers soup, beans, onion, cheese and almonds. Bake at 350° until hot throughout and cheese has melted.

Joan Pharis

HASH BROWN CASSEROLE

2 bags frozen hash browns
1 pt. sour cream
1 can cream of chicken soup
½ c. chopped onion

2 c. grated cheddar cheese
½ c. melted butter or margarine
½ tsp. salt
¼ tsp. pepper

Thaw hash browns. Mix other ingredients. Add to potatoes. Grease lightly a 9 x 13-inch pan. Pour potatoes in pan and bake at 350° for 1 hour.

Alice Anderson

HERBED BROWN RICE

Cook until tender:

¼ c. butter (or some defatted
  chicken broth - Swanson's)
2 c. chopped onion
½ c. chopped celery

3 lg. cloves garlic, minced
1 tsp. dried crushed thyme OR 1 T.
  snipped fresh thyme

Stir in and cook 2 minutes:

2 c. brown rice, uncooked

2 c. mushrooms, chopped

Stir in and cook 45 minutes:

3½ c. chicken or beef broth

Add:

½ c. shredded Parmesan cheese
1 to 2 c. sautéed chicken pieces
  (opt.)

Let stand 5 to 10 minutes before serving. Makes 6 to 8 cups.

Susan Fiske

HOLIDAY SPAGHETTI

½ lb. (8-oz. pkg.) spaghetti, cooked
  until tender & drained
½ c. shortening

1 lg. onion, chopped
1 green pepper, chopped
1 (8-oz.) can mushrooms, drained

Cook above items slowly until tender. Add:

1 lb. ground lean meat
1 (No. 2½ can) peeled tomatoes
3 tsp. salt

1 tsp. sugar
Cooked spaghetti

Transfer to 9 x 2 x 13-inch pan. Sprinkle on grated cheese. Bake 30 minutes at 350°.

Emma Geren

IMPOSSIBLE GREEN CHILI-CHEESE PIE

2 (4-oz.) cans chopped green
  chilies, drained
4 c. (16 oz.) shredded cheddar
  cheese

2 c. milk
4 eggs
1 c. Bisquick baking mix

Heat oven to 425°. Grease pie plate, 10 x 1½ inches. Sprinkle chilies and cheese in plate. Beat remaining ingredients until smooth. Pour into plate. Bake until knife inserted in center comes out clean, about 25 to 30 minutes. Cool 10 minutes before serving.

Joan Pharis

23304-98

ITALIAN DELIGHT

Cook in oil:

1 onion
1 green pepper

2 cloves garlic

Add and brown:

½ lb. hamburger

Add:

1 c. corn
½ c. peas
1 c. Del Monte hot sauce
1 c. Campbell's tomato soup

1 sm. can mushrooms
Salt & pepper to taste
Dash chili powder
Splash Worcestershire sauce

Cook and drain:

½ lb. macaroni

Add cooked ingredients to macaroni. Stir in 1 tablespoon Parmesan cheese. Pour into 9 x 13-inch casserole dish. Sprinkle 1 tablespoon Parmesan cheese on top. Bake in moderate oven for 15 minutes.

Jean Edwards

LASAGNA

8 oz. wide lasagna noodles
¼ c. Parmesan cheese
1 lb. ground beef (opt.)
1 sm. ctn. cottage cheese
2 cans spaghetti sauce with meat (I use Chef Boy-Ar-Dee)

8 oz. Jack (or mozzarella) cheese, grated
¼ tsp. pepper
1 egg, beaten
1 T. parsley flakes
1 tsp. salt

Cook noodles as per direction. Rinse and set aside. Cook ground beef (if using) and combine with spaghetti sauce. Grate the Jack (or mozzarella) cheese. Combine cottage cheese, egg, Parmesan, parsley flakes, salt and pepper. In 9 x 13-inch baking dish layer: half the noodles lengthwise, half the cottage cheese mixture, half the grated Jack or mozzarella, half the spaghetti sauce. Make a second layer of the same. Bake at 375° for 30 to 35 minutes. Let stand 5 minutes before serving.

Note: I have found that putting a thin layer of sauce in the baking dish first prevents the noodles from sticking and getting hard.

Dorothy Anderson

LEFTOVER TURKEY

3 c. diced cooked turkey
2 hard-boiled eggs, chopped
1 (4-oz.) can sliced mushrooms
¾ c. diced celery
½ c. sliced water chestnuts

1 T. chopped onion
1 (10½-oz.) can cream of chicken soup
¾ c. mayonnaise
Crushed potato chips

(continued)

Mix together turkey, eggs, mushrooms, celery, water chestnuts and onion. Stir soup into mayonnaise and toss with turkey mixture. Turn into 2-quart casserole. Sprinkle with chips. Bake, uncovered, at 350° for 30 minutes or until mixture is bubbling. Serves 6.

Marge Todd

LORELY'S SQUASH CASSEROLE

1 lb. (6 or 8) yellow crookneck
  squash
1 onion, chopped
½ c. chopped green pepper
2 T. butter or margarine
Dash salt
Dash pepper

12 saltine crackers, crushed
1½ c. grated cheddar cheese
½ c. mayonnaise
½ c. milk
2 heaping tsp. Dijon mustard
1 egg

Cook squash, onion and green pepper in small amount of water. Drain and add salt, pepper and butter. Pour into casserole dish. Add crackers and ½ of cheese. Mix together slightly beaten egg, mayonnaise, milk and mustard. Add to casserole and mix thoroughly. Cover top with rest of cheese. Bake at 350° for 20 to 30 minutes, until lightly browned and bubbly.

Toni Williams

LOW-FAT STROGANOFF

½ onion, sliced
1 can low-fat cream of mushroom
  soup
1 tsp. garlic powder
1 lb. ground turkey or chicken

1 T. water
½ lb. mushrooms
Sour cream
Noodles, boiled

Sauté onions, mushrooms and garlic in water. Add ground meat and brown. Add soup and sour cream. Heat on low to medium. Serve on noodles.

Wilmanita Rogers

MEXICAN CASSEROLE

1 lb. lean ground beef
1 stalk celery, diced
¼ c. chopped onion
1 (4-oz.) can chopped Ortega green
  chilies
2 (16-oz.) cans Rosarita spicy
  refried beans
1 (4-oz.) can sliced ripe olives

1 lg. tomato, diced
¼ c. chopped onion
Grated sharp cheddar cheese
Crushed restaurant-style tortilla
  chips
½ tsp. salt
½ c. water
1 pkg. taco seasoning

Brown ground beef, celery, onion and salt; drain. Add water, taco seasoning, green chilies and refried beans. Simmer bean mixture as you spray a 2-quart baking dish with Pam. Cover baking dish with crushed tortilla chips, then top with grated cheddar cheese just to cover. Add bean mixture. Bake in 375° oven for 30 minutes. Top casserole with chopped onion, sliced olives, diced tomatoes, grated cheese

(continued)

23304-98

and more crushed tortilla chips. May be served with or without guacamole on the side.

Ellen Fritz Wallace

MEXICAN CASSEROLE

1 lb. ground meat
1 can cream of mushroom soup
1 can cream of chicken soup
1 sm. can Ortega peppers

1 can enchilada sauce
1 pkg. Dorito chips
Grated cheese

Brown meat and pour off excess fat. Add soups, peppers and enchilada sauce. Pour over the Dorito taco chips in 9 x 13-inch pan. Cover top with grated cheese. Bake at 350° for 25 minutes.

Opal Williams

MEXICAN LASAGNA

1½ lbs. ground beef
1 med. onion, chopped
1 clove garlic, minced
1-lb. can chopped tomatoes
1 (10-oz.) can red chili sauce
4-oz. can chopped ripe olives
½ lb. ricotta or cottage cheese
½ lb. shredded med. cheddar
  cheese

1 egg
8 corn tortillas
¼ c. oil
¼ tsp. pepper
1 tsp. salt
½ lb. Jack cheese
Tortilla chips

Brown the meat, onion and garlic. Add tomatoes, chili sauce, olives, salt and pepper. In small skillet heat oil and soften tortillas; drain. (I have skipped the softening of tortillas process with very little difference in the quality.) Shred Jack cheese. Mix ricotta with egg. Spread ⅓ of meat sauce mix in 9 x 13 x 2-inch baking dish. Top with half the ricotta mix. Layer half the tortillas, cut in half. Repeat, reserving ⅓ of the meat sauce for top. Bake at 350° for 20 minutes. Top with tortilla chips. Add the cheddar cheese. Return to oven and heat until cheese is nice and melted. Let stand 5 minutes before serving.

Dorothy Anderson

MEXICAN MEAL

Brown together:

1 lb. ground meat

1 sm. chopped onion

Add:

1 can tomato paste
3 cans water
2 cloves garlic, crushed

1 can tomato sauce
2 T. sugar

Add:

1 tsp. Accent
1 tsp. oregano

1 tsp. chili powder
1 tsp. salt
1 tsp. whole cumin seed

Simmer 40 minutes, then add 1 cup cooked rice. Serve over Fritos or similar chips.
Garnishes: Put in separate bowls and let each choose own garnish: avocado, chopped green onions, sliced tomatoes, chopped olives, grated cheese, shredded lettuce, green chili salsa.

Dressing (this serves 16):

1 (8 oz.) cream cheese
2 c. buttermilk

2 c. mayonnaise

Beat together and add 1 teaspoon each of pepper, salt, onion salt and Accent and 1 crushed garlic clove.

Connie Kinsel

NUTTY RICE PATTIES

1½ c. cooked brown rice
½ c. shredded zucchini
¼ c. whole-wheat flour
1 egg, beaten

1 T. finely chopped parsley
1 T. dry roasted sunflower nuts
⅛ tsp. pepper
2 T. oil

Sweet & Sour Sauce:

2 T. brown sugar
2 tsp. cornstarch
⅓ c. pineapple juice

2 T. cider vinegar
1 T. orange juice

Combine rice, zucchini, flour, egg, parsley, nuts and pepper; mix well. Shape into 6 patties using about ⅓ cup mixture for each. Cook patties in oil in large skillet until golden brown. In small saucepan, combine brown sugar, cornstarch, pineapple juice, vinegar, orange juice. Cook over medium heat until mixture boils and thickens, stirring constantly. Serve over patties.

Joan Pharis

23304-98

ORANGE RICE

1 sm. onion, finely chopped
2 lg. ribs celery
1 orange peel, slivered
1/3 tsp. crushed thyme
1 c. rice

2 T. butter
1 1/2 c. water
1 c. orange juice
Salt to taste

Cook chopped onion gently for 5 minutes. Mix rest of ingredients except rice and bring to a boil. Add rice and stir. Bring to boil again; cover and cook 25 minutes, until moisture is absorbed.

Mildred Walters

PARTY OMELET

12 slices white bread, trimmed
1 cube butter, melted
1 1/2 lbs. cheddar cheese, grated
Green onions
1 1/2 c. milk

1 c. chopped ham
Sliced mushrooms
Sliced olives
6 eggs

Dip 1 slice bread in melted butter and place in bottom of casserole dish. Fill bottom with butter-dipped slices, 6 to 8 slices per layer. Sprinkle with layer of chopped ham, cheddar cheese, mushrooms, olives and green onions. Put in another layer of bread slices and repeat with sprinkles. Top with remaining ham and cheese. Beat the eggs in milk. Pour over mixture. Bake at 350° for 45 minutes. I usually double this recipe.

Alice Anderson

PORK CHOP-CABBAGE SUPPER
(For One or Two)

2 pork loin chops (1/2 inch thick)
1 (10 3/4-oz.) can cream of
  mushroom soup
1/4 tsp. salt

3 c. shredded cabbage
1 T. cooking oil
1/2 tsp. garlic powder
1/4 tsp. pepper

In an ovenproof skillet, brown pork chops in oil on both sides. Remove and set aside. To drippings, add soup and seasonings and bring to a boil. Return chops to skillet and add cabbage. Cover and bake at 350° until meat is tender, 50 to 60 minutes.

Bernette Parvey

REAL TEXAS CHILI

3 lbs. stew meat
5 cloves garlic, mashed
2 tsp. cumin
1 T. leaf oregano
6 tsp. beef bouillon, dried

2 T. oil
5 T. chili powder
1/2 c. flour
Sour cream, light

(continued)

Heat oil in heavy kettle; add meat, stirring frequently with a wooden spoon, until meat changes color but does not brown. Turn off heat and stir in garlic. Combine chili powder, cumin seed and flour; sprinkle meat with chili mixture until meat is evenly coated. Crumble oregano over meat. Carefully add 6 cups water to beef bouillon. Bring to a boil, stirring occasionally. Reduce heat to low and simmer with vents open for 2 hours or until meat is almost falling apart. Stir occasionally. Cool thoroughly. Cover; **refrigerate overnight to ripen flavor.** Reheat and garnish with sour cream to serve.

Cindi Rogers

RICE CASSEROLE

2 c. brown rice	1 c. boiling water
1 can cream of mushroom soup	1/2 c. hot water
1 (4-oz.) can mushrooms	1/8 tsp. celery salt
1/8 tsp. garlic	1/8 tsp. onion
1/8 tsp. pepper	1/2 tsp. salt
3 T. chopped onion	3 bay leaves
1/2 lb. ground beef	3 T. oil

Put washed rice in pan; cover with boiling water. Brown meat in oil with onion until meat is crumbly. Put soup in bowl with mushrooms, juice, water and seasonings. Add meat. Drain rice and add to meat mixture. Bake 1 hour at 350°.

Wilda Perkins

SAUSAGE & ZUCCHINI SPAGHETTI

1 1/2 lbs. light pork sausage	Dash salt & pepper
2 cans cream of chicken soup	1 1/2 lbs. spaghetti
5 c. zucchini, quartered & sliced	Parmesan cheese, grated
1 lg. onion, chopped	

Cook onion with sausage until the sausage loses its pink color, breaking it up into small pieces. Drain off grease. Stir in soup, zucchini, salt and pepper. Cover and cook over medium heat, stirring occasionally, until zucchini is tender, about 15 minutes. Meanwhile, cook spaghetti noodles until tender; drain. Toss sausage mixture with cooked noodles. Top with Parmesan cheese.

Cindi Rogers

SCALLOPED DINNER

4 potatoes, peeled & sliced	1 lg. onion
4 to 5 carrots, peeled & sliced	1 lb. hamburger
1 pkg. frozen peas	Flour, salt & pepper

Grease deep casserole dish. Place half of potatoes in bottom; sprinkle with flour, salt and pepper. Next layer: thinly sliced onion. Middle layer: brown and season hamburger in frying pan, then layer all of it in casserole dish. Reverse layers:

(continued)

onions, peas and carrots, then potatoes on top, flouring and seasoning. Add milk until it can be seen. Bake at 350° for 1 hour. Ingredients may be varied as needed.

Note: The recipe for this family favorite came from a Mariners dinner served at the First Presbyterian Church of Phoenix, Arizona in 1946.

Eleanor Fritz

SONORA CHICKEN CASSEROLE

4 c. chicken or turkey meat,
  cooked & chopped
2 cans cream of chicken soup,
  condensed
15 oz. chili without beans
4 oz. chili salsa
  green

$\frac{1}{2}$ c. milk
1 sm. onion, chopped fine
12 corn tortillas
$\frac{1}{2}$ lb. Colby cheese, shredded
$\frac{1}{2}$ lb. Monterey Jack cheese,
  shredded

In a large bowl, combine condensed soups, chili, chili salsa, milk and onion. In large shallow casserole, put a layer of half of the chicken or turkey; cover with half the tortillas torn into small pieces. Spread half the sauce over the tortillas, followed by half the cheeses. Repeat these layers, ending with the cheeses. To bake immediately, put into 350° oven for about 45 minutes. Let it stand 10 minutes before serving. If you freeze this, reheat it for 90 minutes and check the deep middle before serving.

Cindi Rogers

SOUR CREAM ENCHILADA

1 sm. chicken
1 can chopped green chilies
1 can cream of chicken soup

1 (8 oz.) sour cream
12 tortillas
1 lb. cheddar cheese

Boil and bone chicken. Mix all ingredients except $\frac{1}{2}$ cheese. Dip tortillas in hot oil; roll mix in them. Place in baking pan. Pour remainder over top and cover with rest of cheese. Add some chicken broth to moisten. Bake at 400° for 5 to 10 minutes, until heated through.

Joyce O'Neal

SPICY BLACK BEANS & TOMATOES

1 tsp. olive oil
$\frac{1}{2}$ c. chopped onion
2 cloves garlic, minced
2 ($14\frac{1}{2}$-oz.) cans no-salt-added
  whole tomatoes, drained &
  chopped
2 T. canned chopped green chilies

$\frac{1}{2}$ tsp. ground cumin
2 (15-oz.) cans black beans,
  rinsed & drained
$\frac{1}{2}$ tsp. ground red pepper
$\frac{1}{4}$ tsp. chili powder
1 T. chopped fresh cilantro

Coat a large skillet with cooking spray. Add oil. Place over medium heat until hot. Add onion and garlic and sauté until tender. Add tomato and green chilies. Reduce heat and cook, uncovered, 6 to 8 minutes or until mixture is slightly thickened, stirring occasionally. Stir in beans and remaining ingredients. Cover and cook 5

(continued)

minutes or until thoroughly heated. Good served with rice. 105 calories and 9% fat per ½-cup serving.

Joan Pharis

SPINACH-BROCCOLI CASSEROLE

3 (10-oz.) pkgs. chopped frozen spinach
3 (10-oz.) pkgs. frozen broccoli

1 pt. sour cream
1 pkg. dry onion soup mix
Cheddar cheese

Cook spinach and broccoli and drain well. Mix soup and sour cream, then fold in veggies. Sprinkle cheddar cheese on top. Bake, uncovered, until heated through and cheese melts.

Joan Pharis

SPINACH & CHEESE QUICHE

Line a quiche pan with pie crust and partially bake. (I have found that Betty Crocker ready-crust works perfectly.)

10-oz. pkg. frozen chopped spinach, cooked, drained & dry
¼ tsp. salt
Pepper

1 tsp. horseradish
4 T. sour cream
½ c. grated Swiss cheese
3 T. grated Parmesan cheese

Spread ingredients over bottom of pie crust.

Custard:

4 eggs
¾ c. milk
¾ c. heavy cream
2 T. melted butter

1 T. flour
Pinch salt
Pinch nutmeg
Pinch cayenne pepper

Beat together custard ingredients and spread over spinach and cheese. Bake at 375° for 40 minutes.

Joyce O'Neal

SQUASH CASSEROLE

1 lb. cooked squash
1 can cream of chicken soup
1 c. green onions, chopped
½ pkg. herb stuffing

1 stick melted margarine
½ qt. sour cream
Salt & pepper

Combine all ingredients and place in baking dish. Bake 30 minutes at 350°, uncovered.

Joan Pharis

23304-98

SWEDISH CABBAGE ROLLS

12 lg. cabbage leaves, separated & parboiled for 5 minutes
1 lb. ground beef
1 c. cooked rice
2/3 c. milk
1/4 c. onion, divided
2 T. brown sugar
1 can condensed tomato soup
4 cloves
1 tsp. parsley, chopped (opt.)
1 egg
1 tsp. salt
1/8 tsp. pepper
1/2 can water
1 bay leaf

Drain cabbage leaves and trim out the thick center vein. Combine ground meat, rice, parsley, egg, milk, half the onion, salt and pepper. Place a spoonful on each cabbage leaf and roll up. Fasten with a toothpick. Place in a baking dish. Sprinkle with sugar and cover with soup and water. Add remaining onion, bay leaf, and cloves. Bake, uncovered, in moderate oven (325°) about 1 1/2 hours. Add more water if needed.

Toni Williams

TAMALE PIE

4 lg. XLent tamales (other brands OK, cut them up)
1 lg. can corn with juice
1 (6-oz.) can tomato paste
1 can Dennisons chili con carne, WITHOUT beans
1 can chopped or sliced olives, drained

Mix and bake 45 minutes to 1 hour at 350° in a 2 1/2-quart casserole dish.

Betty Baird

TAMALE PIE

1/2 lb. ground beef
1/2 c. celery, chopped
1/2 bell pepper, chopped
1 garlic clove, mashed or chopped
1 c. tofu, cut in cubes
1/4 c. black olives, whole or chopped
1/2 tsp. ground coriander
1 to 2 T. chili powder
1/2 onion, chopped
Oil, for sautéing
1 c. water or milk
1/2 c. cornmeal
1 c. canned tomatoes
Salt to taste
Pepper to taste

Sauté the onions, pepper, celery, garlic in the oil until onions look clear. Add ground beef and tofu and sauté a few minutes longer. Add cornmeal, water, tomatoes, olives, salt and pepper, chili powder and coriander. Pour into casserole. Bake in 350° oven about 45 minutes, until brown, bubbly and well blended. This recipe allows you to cut your meat and cholesterol consumption in half without sacrificing flavor.

Ruth Wills

TAMALE PIE CASSEROLE

1 lg. onion, chopped
1 lg. can tomatoes
1 can corn
3 tsp. chili powder

1 can olives
½ c. oil
1 lb. ground round

Mix together and boil 15 minutes; remove from fire. Beat 2 eggs. Add to ½ cup or a little more cornmeal and ½ cup milk. Add to first mixture. Place in casserole dish. Cook at 350° for 45 minutes. This is quick and easy!

Ruth Caudill

THANK OFFERING TURKEY DRESSING

1 pkg. Mrs. Cubbison's seasoned
  cornbread
1 pkg. bread cubes
1½ c. chopped celery
1 med. onion
2 eggs, beaten

2½ c. water or chicken broth
1 pkg. Farmer John sausage, cut
  into sm. pieces
1½ tsp. poultry seasoning
1 tsp. sage

Mix all the above ingredients together. Bake in 4-quart casserole for approximately 1½ hours at 325°-350°.

Presbyterian Women's Group

TOFU MEAT LOAF

¾ lb. ground beef
¼ lb. ground sausage (opt.)
1⅔ c. tofu
1 med. onion, chopped fine
½ c. celery, chopped
¼ c. parsley

2 eggs (or 1 egg if desired)
½ c. wheat germ (opt.)
¼ c. milk
⅓ c. sunflower seeds (opt.)
Other seasoning*

Combine all ingredients except sunflower seeds in a bowl and beat with an electric mixer until smooth. Spoon the mixture into a loaf pan and top with sunflower seeds. Bake for 1 to 1½ hours at 350°. This recipe allows you to cut your meat and cholesterol consumption in half without sacrificing flavor. *Seasoning of your choice can be added to meat loaf prior to baking.

Ruth Wills

TOSTADA GRANDE

2 pkgs. biscuits, refrigerated
6 oz. corn chips, crushed
8 oz. sour cream, light
8 oz. creamy Italian dressing
1½ T. flour
2½ c. turkey, cooked & chopped

4 oz. green chilies, drained &
  chopped
4 oz. olives, chopped
Lettuce, shredded
Cheese, shredded
Tomatoes, chopped

Preheat oven to 400°. Pat biscuits into bottom of 15½ x 10½ x 1-inch pan. Sprinkle with corn chips, mounding on sides. Bake 10 minutes. Meanwhile, in large bowl,

(continued)

23304-98

blend sour cream, creamy Italian dressing and flour; add turkey, chilies and olives. Spread evenly on crust, leaving 1-inch border. Bake an additional 7 minutes or until edges are brown. Garnish with lettuce, cheese and tomato.

Cindi Rogers

TWO-CORN CASSEROLE

3 (No. 1) cans hominy
2 (12-oz.) cans whole-kernel corn
1 (4-oz.) can diced green chili
$\frac{1}{2}$ pt. or more sour cream

$\frac{1}{2}$ c. shredded Jack cheese
Dash salt
Dash pepper
$\frac{1}{2}$ stick butter

Rinse and drain hominy. Butter a 2-quart casserole. Layer $\frac{1}{3}$ hominy in bottom, then $\frac{1}{3}$ corn. Add a generous grind of black pepper, a touch of salt and 3 tablespoons diced chili. Dot with butter and add 4 tablespoons sour cream and $\frac{1}{2}$ cup cheese. Repeat layers, ending with last $\frac{1}{3}$ of hominy and corn and top with dabs of butter and cheese on top. Bake at 350° for 35 to 40 minutes.

Fran Delano

VEGETABLE LASAGNA

3 c. grated zucchini
3 c. grated carrots
1 c. grated Parmesan cheese
$2\frac{1}{2}$ c. spaghetti sauce
2 (10-oz.) pkgs. frozen chopped
  spinach, thawed & drained

$\frac{1}{2}$ lb. lasagna noodles, cooked
8 oz. shredded provolone cheese
3 lg. eggs
1 T. olive oil

Sauté zucchini and carrots separately in $\frac{1}{2}$ tablespoon oil each until tender but crisp. Combine eggs and Parmesan. In 3 bowls stir $\frac{1}{3}$ egg mixture separately into spinach, carrots and zucchini. Layer noodles, vegetables and provolone cheese. Top with noodles and sauce; cover with foil. Bake at 350° for 30 minutes. Remove foil and sprinkle with more provolone. Bake 10 minutes longer. Cool 10 minutes before cutting.

Joyce O'Neal

VEGETABLE-NOODLE CASSEROLE

1 ($10\frac{3}{4}$-oz.) can cream of chicken
  soup, undiluted
1 ($10\frac{3}{4}$-oz.) can cream of broccoli
  soup, undiluted
$1\frac{1}{2}$ c. milk
1 c. grated Parmesan cheese,
  divided
3 garlic cloves, minced

2 T. dried parsley flakes
$\frac{1}{2}$ tsp. pepper
$\frac{1}{4}$ tsp. salt
1 (16-oz.) pkg. wide egg noodles,
  cooked & drained
1 (16-oz.) pkg. frozen broccoli,
  cauliflower & carrot blend, thawed
2 c. frozen corn, thawed

In a bowl, combine soup, milk, $\frac{3}{4}$ cup Parmesan cheese, garlic, parsley, pepper and salt. Mix well. Add noodles and vegetables; mix well. Pour into a greased 13 x 9 x 2-inch baking dish. Sprinkle with the remaining Parmesan. Cover and bake at 350° for 45 to 50 minutes or until heated through. Yields 12 to 14 servings.

Erma Donaldson

VIVA LA CHICKEN

4 chicken breasts, wrapped in
 foil & baked 1 hour at 375°

Cool, skin, cut meat in bite-sized pieces. Mix:

1 can cream of mushroom soup
1 can cream of chicken soup
1 can green chili salsa

1 c. milk
1 T. dry onion flakes

Butter 13 x 9-inch Pyrex dish. Tear up 3 tortillas and place in bottom of dish. Add:

¼ lb. grated cheese
½ chicken

½ sauce

Repeat with 3 more tortillas, cheese, chicken and remainder of sauce. Top with more cheese (use ¾ to 1 pound total). Refrigerate 24 hours (if convenient). Bake at 350° for 35 to 45 minutes.

Mildred Walters

Recipe Favorites

23304-98

Meat,
Poultry
&
Seafood

Helpful Hints

• When preparing sauces and marinades for red meats, use little oil. Fat from the meat will render out during cooking and will provide plenty of flavor. Certain meats, like ribs, pot roast, sausage and others, can be parboiled before grilling to reduce the fat content.

• When shopping for red meats, buy the leanest cuts you can find. Fat will show up as an opaque white coating, and it can also run through the meat fibers themselves, as marbling. Although much outer fat (the white coating) can be trimmed away, there isn't much to be done about the marbling. Stay away from well marbled cuts of meat.

• Home from work late with no time for marinating meat? Pound meat lightly with a mallet or rolling pin. Pierce with a fork and sprinkle lightly with meat tenderizer and add marinade. Refrigerate for about 20 minutes and you will have succulent, tender meat.

• Marinating is a cinch if you use a plastic bag. The meat stays in the marinade and it's easy to turn and rearrange. Cleanup is easy. Just toss the bag.

• Meat may slice more thinly if it is partially frozen.

• Tomatoes added to roasts will help tenderize them naturally. Tomatoes contain an acid that works well to break down meats.

• Always cut meats across the grain when possible; they will be easier to eat and have a better appearance.

• When frying meat, try sprinkling paprika over it and it will turn golden brown.

• Thaw all meats in the refrigerator for maximum safety.

• Refrigerate poultry promptly after purchasing. Keep it in the coldest section of your refrigerator for up to two days. For longer storage, freeze the poultry. Never leave poultry at room temperature for more than two hours.

• If you're microwaving skinned chicken, be sure to cover the baking dish with vented clear plastic wrap to keep the chicken moist.

• Lemon juice rubbed on fish before cooking will enhance the flavor and help maintain a good color.

• To make scaling a fish easier, try rubbing vinegar on the scales first.

MEATS, FISH & POULTRY

ANN LANDERS' MEAT LOAF

2 lbs. ground beef
1½ c. bread crumbs
1 tsp. Accent
1 pkg. Lipton onion soup mix
1 (8-oz.) can tomato sauce

2 eggs
¾ c. ketchup
2 c. WARM water
2 strips bacon

Mix beef, bread crumbs, eggs, ketchup, Accent, water and soup mix thoroughly. Put into loaf pan. Cover with bacon strips and tomato sauce. Bake 1 hour at 350°.

Fran Delano

BAR-B-QUE BEEF SANDWICHES

4 c. cooked beef (or use leftover roast)
1½ c. water
¼ c. granulated sugar
4 tsp. prepared mustard
¼ tsp. pepper
¼ tsp. cayenne pepper
2 thick lemon slices

1 c. chili sauce (or catsup)
1 T. Worcestershire sauce
¼ c. vinegar
1 T. salt
2 onions, sliced
1 cube margarine
Hamburger buns

Combine all ingredients except chili sauce (or catsup) and Worcestershire sauce. Simmer 20 minutes. Add the chili sauce (catsup) and Worcestershire sauce. Serve between hamburger buns. Serves 8+.

Dot Anderson

BEEF & PEPPER MEDLEY

2 T. garlic powder
2 T. cracked black pepper
1 eye of round beef roast (about 4 lbs.)

2 lg. green peppers, julienned
2 lg. sweet red peppers, julienned
2 lg. sweet onions, cut into thin wedges

Dressing:

⅔ c. olive or vegetable oil
½ c. red wine vinegar
2 T. Dijon mustard

2 garlic cloves, minced
½ tsp. crushed red pepper flakes

Combine garlic powder and pepper. Rub over all sides of roast. Place on a rack in a shallow roasting pan. Preheat oven to 500°. Place roast in oven and reduce heat to 350°. Bake for 1½ to 2 hours or until meat reaches desired doneness. Chill for 30 to 40 minutes or until meat is cool enough to handle. Cut into 3 x ¼ x ¼-inch strips. Place in a large salad bowl. Add peppers and onions. Combine dressing ingredients in a jar with tight-fitting lid and shake well. Pour over salad and toss to coat. Cover and refrigerate overnight. Serve cold. Yields 10 to 12 servings.

Erma Donaldson

CHINESE BEEF & RICE

⅔ c. rice
2 stalks celery, chopped
1 green pepper, chopped
1 med. onion, chopped
1 beef bouillon cube

2 T. oil
1½ tsp. salt
1½ c. boiling water
2 tsp. soy sauce

Cook rice in hot oil over medium heat until golden brown. Add salt, water, bouillon cube and soy sauce. Cover and simmer 20 minutes. Add the rest of the ingredients. Cover tightly and simmer 10 minutes more. (It may be necessary to add a little more water.) All water should be absorbed; if not, remove cover and allow liquid to evaporate. Serve. Cooked chicken or pork can be used in place of beef. Makes 2 generous servings.

Barbara Lockridge

PORCUPINE MEATBALLS

½ c. uncooked long-grain rice
⅓ c. chopped onion
½ tsp. celery salt
⅛ tsp. garlic powder
2 T. cooking oil
1 (15-oz.) can tomato sauce
2 tsp. Worcestershire sauce

½ c. water
1 tsp. salt
⅛ tsp. pepper
1 lb. ground beef
1 c. water
2 T. brown sugar

In a bowl, combine rice, water, onion, salt, celery salt, pepper and garlic powder. Add beef and mix well. Shape into 1½-inch balls. In a large skillet, brown meatballs in oil; drain. Combine tomato sauce, water, brown sugar and Worcestershire sauce. Pour over meatballs. Reduce heat; cover and simmer for 1 hour. Yields 4 to 6 servings.

Erma Donaldson

PORK CHOPS

1 onion, chopped
½ c. catsup
1 tsp. hot pepper sauce (I use ¼ c. or more salsa)

¼ c. water
2 T. white vinegar
1 T. molasses

Trim and brown 6 pork chops and put into a Pyrex dish (I don't brown). Add above sauce mixture and bake 45 minutes at 350°.

Betty Baird

PRIME RIB

3-rib roast of beef (without short ribs)
Flour

Salt
Coarsely cracked black pepper

Preheat oven to 500°. Remove roast from refrigerator (not room temperature) and place in a shallow, open roasting pan. Sprinkle with flour and rub into meat.

(continued)

23304-98

Season generously with salt and pepper. Place a tent of aluminum foil loosely over the top of the roast to protect the oven from splattered fat. Place in extremely hot oven and roast as follows: 8 minutes per pound for rare, 9 minutes per pound for medium, 10 minutes per pound for well done. When roasting time is up, **turn off oven heat, but do not open open door.** Let roast remain in the oven at least 1 hour. (Standing time and individual oven differences will determine degree of rareness in center of roast.)

Cindi Rogers

SAVORY MEAT IN GRAVY

2 lbs. ground beef, extra lean
1 lg. onion, finely chopped
6 tsp. beef bouillon, dried

¾ c. flour
6 bay leaves
½ tsp. nutmeg

Brown ground beef with onion. Add 4 cups water, beef bouillon, bay leaves and nutmeg. Bring to boil; cover and simmer for ½ hour. Combine the flour with 2 additional cups of water, mixing thoroughly. Remove bay leaves from simmering meat, then add flour mixture. Stir gently until thickened. Serve over mashed potatoes.

Cindi Rogers

STUFFED BEEF LOG

2 lbs. ground beef
½ c. quick-cooking oats
½ c. finely chopped onion
⅓ tsp. pepper (or season to your taste)

½ c. milk
1 egg, beaten
2 tsp. salt

Combine ingredients and mix thoroughly. Shape into rectangle about 10 x 16 inches on aluminum foil. Spread Sausage Stuffing evenly over meat. Roll as for a jellyroll and place, seam side down, on rack in open roasting pan. Bake in moderate oven (300°) for 1 hour and 15 minutes.

Sausage Stuffing:

½ lb. pork sausage (fresh)
1 med. potato, grated fine
½ grated onion

1 egg
1 c. soft bread crumbs
½ tsp. salt

Combine ingredients and mix well.

Alice Anderson

STUFFED GREEN PEPPERS

3 lg. peppers
1 c. boiling water, salted (1½ tsp.)
½ lb. ground beef
1 (8-oz.) can tomato sauce
1 T. chopped onion

½ c. coarse dry bread or cracker crumbs
1 tsp. salt
¼ tsp. pepper

(continued)

Heat oven to 350°. Cut a thin slice from the stem end of each pepper. Wash outside and inside. Remove seeds and membranes. Cook peppers in boiling, salted water for 5 minutes; drain. Mix rest of ingredients. Stuff peppers lightly with mixture. Stand upright in small baking dish. Bake, covered, for 45 minutes. Uncover and bake 15 minutes more. Yields 2 to 3 servings.

Barbara Lockridge

SWEET & SOUR PORK

1 lb. boneless lean pork, cut into ¾-inch cubes
½ med.-sized yellow onion, peeled & cut into 1-inch squares with layers separated

1 sm. bell pepper, seeded & cut into 1-inch squares
1 sm. carrot, peeled & sliced
¾ c. pineapple chunks
4 c. oil for deep-frying

Marinade:

½ tsp. salt
½ tsp. garlic powder

1 T. dry sherry
1 egg white

Coating for Meat:

½ c. flour

½ c. cornstarch

Combine marinade ingredients in a medium bowl. Add pork and mix well, then set aside for 30 minutes. Combine Sweet and Sour Sauce and set aside. (Do not thicken the sauce until later.) Coat marinated pork with the flour and cornstarch blend. Heat oil to 350° and deep-fry pork for about 3 minutes or until golden brown. Remove pork and drain on paper towels. Reheat Sweet and Sour Sauce. Stir until sauce boils and then thickens with a mixture of 2 tablespoons cornstarch plus 3 tablespoons water. Stir in bell pepper, yellow onion, carrot and pineapple. Bring to a boil; stir in cooked pork. Mix well and serve.

Sweet and Sour Sauce:

½ c. sugar
¼ c. catsup
¼ c. pineapple juice
½ tsp. ginger powder

¼ c. cider vinegar
1 c. water
1 tsp. fresh lemon juice
Red coloring (opt.)

Mix all the ingredients in a pot. Bring to a boil over medium-high heat, stirring occasionally. Thicken with a mixture of 2 tablespoons cornstarch plus 3 tablespoons of water.

Jay Sue

SWEET & SOUR STIR-FRY

2 T. cornstarch
2 T. oil
1 lg. red bell pepper, seeded & cut in 1-inch pieces (2 c.)
12 oz. boned & skinned chicken breasts, cut in 1½-inch chunks
8 oz. fresh sugar-snap peas, trimmed
2½ c. or 1 (9-oz.) box frozen sugar-snap peas
1 (8-oz.) can sliced water chestnuts, drained
¾ c. bottled sweet & sour stir-fry sauce
Sliced scallions, for garnish

Put cornstarch in a plastic food bag. Add chicken and toss to coat. Heat oil in a large (preferably nonstick) skillet over medium-high heat until hot but not smoking. Add chicken and stir-fry 3 to 4 minutes, until golden brown on all sides. Remove to a bowl with a slotted spoon. Add bell pepper, snap peas and water chestnuts to drippings in skillet. Stir-fry 2 to 3 minutes or until vegetables are crisp-tender. Pour in stir-fry sauce and return chicken to skillet. Stir to coat chicken and vegetables. Garnish with scallions. **Alternatives:** Leave out water chestnuts and add almonds, peanuts or cashews. Add drained, canned pineapple chunks. Add ½ teaspoon crushed red pepper.

Barbara Lockridge

SWEDISH MEATBALLS

4 eggs
8 slices white bread, torn
¼ c. finely chopped onion
1 to 2 tsp. salt
2 T. shortening
1 (12-oz.) can evaporated milk
2 (10¾-oz.) cans cream of chicken soup
2 (10¾-oz.) cans cream of mushroom soup, undiluted
1 c. milk
2 lbs. ground beef
4 tsp. baking powder
1 tsp. pepper
Minced fresh parsley

In a large bowl, beat eggs and milk. Add bread and mix gently. Let stand for 5 minutes. Add beef, onion, baking powder, salt and pepper. Mix well (mixture will be soft). Shape into 1-inch balls. In a large skillet, brown meatballs, a few at a time, in shortening. Place in an ungreased 3-quart baking dish. In a bowl, stir soups and milk until smooth. Pour over meatballs. Bake, uncovered, at 350° for 1 hour. Sprinkle with parsley. Yields 8 to 10 servings.

Erma Donaldson

VENISON POT ROAST

1 boneless shoulder venison roast
  (3 to 4 lbs.)
3 T. cooking oil
1 (14½-oz.) can chicken broth

⅓ c. soy sauce
1 lg. onion, sliced
4 garlic cloves, minced
½ tsp. ground ginger

Spaetzle:

2 eggs
½ tsp. salt
2¼ c. all-purpose flour
⅔ c. milk

2 qt. beef broth
¼ c. butter or margarine, melted
⅛ tsp. pepper

Gravy:

⅓ c. water

⅓ c. flour

In a Dutch oven, brown roast in oil. Add the next 5 ingredients. Cover and simmer for 4 hours or until meat is tender. For spaetzle, beat eggs and salt in a medium bowl. With a wooden spoon, gradually stir in flour and milk. In a large saucepan, bring broth to a boil. Place dough in a colander or spaetzle maker. Place over boiling broth. Press dough with a wooden spoon until bits drop into broth. Cook for 5 minutes or until tender; drain. Toss spaetzle with butter. Sprinkle with pepper and keep warm. Remove roast to a serving platter and keep warm. Measure 3 cups pan juices and return to pan. Combine water and flour; stir into pan juices. Cook and stir until thickened and bubbly. Cook and stir 1 minute more. Slice roast. Serve with spaetzle and gravy.

Erma Donaldson

FISH THE EASY WAY

Spread fillet (cod, snapper, etc.) out in a baking pan. Cover with nonfat milk, salt and pepper. Sprinkle with dill weed. Bake at 400° for 15 to 20 minutes. This is a nonfat dish!

Betty Baird

HALIBUT IN MAYONNAISE SAUCE

1 pkg. Pepperidge Farm puff pastry
  shells

1 lb. halibut
1 c. mayonnaise

White Sauce:

2 T. butter
1 c. milk
Dash pepper

2 T. flour
½ tsp. salt

Bake puff pastry following the directions on the box. Cool and remove top of pastry and clean any pastry from inside. Broil halibut; cool, bone and break into chunks. Prepare white sauce in a double boiler, cooking until thick. Add mayonnaise and blend. Add chunks of cooked, boned halibut. Fill pastry cups with halibut-white sauce mix. Dot with butter and broil until lightly browned. Serves 4 to 6.

Kathie Gifford

23304-98

LOBSTER

Use fresh or frozen lobster. Split lobster down back, starting at tail end; pull back with thumbs. Slice thumbs under meat; pull out. Put shell together. Place shells on cookie sheet or pie pan. Place lobster meat on top of shell and brush with butter. Bake at 250°-275°. Check in 15 minutes for pink color. Lobster is done when it turns pink (don't let it get too dry). Melt butter in small cup or bowl. Serve.

Wilmanita Roberts

SEAFOOD BISQUE

If you make this in the morning, add the wine just before you are ready to serve. Serve on toast points (made ahead) in soup bowls. Makes 2½ quarts or about 8 generous servings.

¾ c. butter	2 c. minced clams
½ c. instant-type all-purpose flour	1 qt. milk
½ pt. cream	4 to 5 green onions
½ lb. sm. bay shrimp	¾ lb. crab meat
½ c. dry white wine	¼ c. pale dry sherry

Garnish:

Parsley

Condiments:

Sieved hard-cooked egg yolks & egg whites (about 4)	½ c. chopped chives
	½ c. chopped macadamia nuts

Melt half of the butter in a large heavy-bottomed pan. Blend in flour and cook about 2 minutes. Drain liquid from clams and stir in the liquid. Stir until blended; reserve clams. Slowly stir in milk and cream and cook until sauce is thickened. Chop the onions finely, discarding half the green part. Sauté onions in remaining butter, cooking until limp. Add crab, shrimp and clams and cook in the butter, stirring lightly, until seafood is hot throughout. Add seafood to the soup mixture and stir in the wine. Heat just until hot. Garnish with parsley. Surround with small bowls of condiments. **Toast Points:** Make ahead. Cut off crusts on thin-sliced white bread and butter on one side. Place, buttered side up, into muffin tins. Bake at 350° until slightly toasted. Place 1 or 2 into soup bowls and ladle Bisque on top.

Susan Fiske

TUNA-CHEESE OPEN FACERS

2 (6½-oz.) cans tuna, drained	1 c. (8 oz.) refrigerated biscuits
1 hard-boiled egg	⅓ c. celery
½ tsp. mustard	2 T. mayonnaise
1 c. (4 oz.) shredded cheddar cheese	

In a small bowl, combine tuna, celery, egg, mayonnaise, mustard and ½ cup of cheese. Separate biscuit dough into 10 biscuits. Pat out each biscuit to a 4-inch circle on 2 lightly greased cookie sheets. Spoon about ¼ cup mixture over each

(continued)

biscuit. Sprinkle with remaining cheese. Bake at 400° for 10 to 13 minutes, until crust is golden brown. Makes 10 sandwiches.

Fran Delano

TUNA-COTTAGE CHEESE SANDWICHES

1 c. cottage cheese, low-fat
7 oz. tuna, packed in water, drained
½ c. mayonnaise, imitation, no cholesterol

2 tsp. taco sauce

Combine ingredients. Use as spread on bread. This is also good on lettuce leaves to use as a salad.

Cindi Rogers

CHICKEN BOMBAY

2½ lbs. breast of chicken, raw, cut bite-sized
1 T. vegetable oil
1 (10-oz.) can Campbell's tomato soup

¼ c. chopped onion
1 med. clove garlic, minced
1 tsp. curry powder
¼ tsp. thyme, crushed

Toppings:

Slivered almonds
Sliced green onions

Raisins, chutney &/or flaked coconut (opt.)

In skillet, brown chicken in oil. Pour off any fat. Add soup, onion, garlic, curry powder and thyme. Cover and simmer 20 minutes or until tender, stirring occasionally. Serve over cooked rice with toppings of your choice.

Susan Fiske

CHICKEN BREASTS DIANE

4 lg. boneless chicken breast halves or 8 sm.
½ tsp. salt
¼ to ½ tsp. black pepper
2 T. olive or salad oil
2 T. butter or margarine
3 T. chopped fresh chives or green onions

Juice of ½ lime or lemon
2 T. brandy or cognac (opt.)
3 T. chopped parsley
2 tsp. Dijon-style mustard
¼ c. chicken broth

Place chicken breast halves between sheets of waxed paper or plastic wrap. Pound slightly with mallet. Sprinkle with salt and pepper. Heat 1 tablespoon each of oil and butter in large skillet. Cook chicken over high heat for 4 minutes on each side. Do not cook longer or they will be overcooked and dry. Transfer to warm serving platter. Add chives or green onion, lime juice and brandy (optional), parsley and mustard to pan. Cook 15 seconds. Whisk in remaining butter and oil. Pour sauce

(continued)

23304-98

over chicken. Serve immediately. Good with noodles and tomato sauce, steamed broccoli and fresh salad. Serves 4.

Barbara Lockridge

CHICKEN & RICE DISH

1 can cream of chicken soup
1 can cream of celery soup
1 can mushroom soup

1 c. raw rice
2 c. chicken broth or bouillon
cubes

Mix all ingredients well. Put in 9 x 13-inch casserole dish. Salt and pepper chicken pieces. Place on top of soup mixture. Bake at 325° for 1 hour. Quick, easy and delicious. I use skinless, boneless chicken breast, but thighs or a whole chicken, cut up, works just as well.

Barbara Lockridge

CHICKEN DIVAN

1 cooked chicken, diced
1 head broccoli, cut up, or 1
   (10-oz.) pkg. frozen broccoli
1 c. sour cream
1 c. mayonnaise
1 can cream of mushroom soup

1 can cream of chicken soup
1 tsp. curry powder
1 T. lemon juice
1 c. grated cheddar cheese
½ c. bread crumbs

Cook broccoli until almost done. Mix together sour cream, mayonnaise, soups, curry powder and lemon juice; set aside. In a 9 x 13-inch pan, layer chicken, broccoli, sauce mixture and grated cheese. Top with bread crumbs. Bake at 350° for 45 minutes or until heated through.

Alice Fritz Gerber

KING RANCH CHICKEN

1 chicken (or equivalent parts),
   boiled & cubed (save the broth)
1 onion, chopped
1 bell pepper, chopped
1 tsp. chili powder
1 can cream of chicken soup,
   undiluted

1 can cream of mushroom soup,
   undiluted
12 oz. mild cheddar cheese, grated
1 can Ro-Tel tomatoes with chili
   peppers
Flour or corn tortillas (I prefer corn
   because flour tends to turn pasty)

Mix chicken, onion and bell pepper together. Mix chili powder and soups together. Break up tortillas and soften in chicken broth, then make a layer in bottom of 9 x 13-inch pan. Make a layer of chicken mixture. Make a layer of cheese. Repeat layers again. On top add soups. Pour Ro-Tel tomatoes on top, then add more cheese. Bake at 350° for 30 to 40 minutes.

Eleanor Fritz

LEMON TERIYAKI-GLAZED CHICKEN

1/2 c. lemon juice
1/4 c. sugar
2 T. water
3/4 tsp. ground ginger
8 thicken thighs (or 4 chicken
  breasts)

1/2 c. soy sauce
3 T. brown sugar
1/2 tsp. garlic powder

In skillet, combine all ingredients except chicken. Cook over medium heat 3 to 4 minutes. Add chicken. Simmer 30 minutes or until thoroughly cooked.

Note: I like to serve Oriental-style vegetables and Rice-A-Roni fried rice on the side.

Ellen Fritz Wallace

MARINATED THANKSGIVING TURKEY

1 1/2 c. chicken broth
1 c. soy sauce
2 garlic cloves, minced
1 1/2 tsp. ground ginger

2 c. water
2/3 c. lemon juice
1 tsp. pepper
1 (12 to 13-lb.) turkey

Combine the broth, water, soy sauce, lemon juice, cloves, ginger and pepper; reserve 1 cup of mixture for basting. Pour remaining marinade into a 2-gallon resealable plastic bag. Add the turkey and seal bag; turn to coat. Refrigerate overnight, turning several times. Drain and discard marinade. Heat grill according to manufacturer's directions for indirect cooking or roast in a conventional oven. Tuck wings under turkey and place with breast side down on grill rack. Cover and grill for 1 hour. Add 10 briquettes to coals. Turn the turkey breast side up. Brush with reserved marinade. Cover and cook for 2 hours, adding 10 briquettes to maintain heat and brushing with marinade every 30 minutes, until meat thermometer reads 185°. Cover and let stand 20 minutes before carving. **Conventional Roasting Method:** Place turkey on a rack in a large roaster. Bake, uncovered, at 325° for 4 to 4 1/2 hours or until meat thermometer reads 185°. Baste frequently with reserved marinade. When turkey begins to brown, cover lightly with a tent of aluminum foil.

Erma Donaldson

NO PEEKING CHICKEN

1 can cream of chicken soup
1 can celery soup
2 c. uncooked rice
1 sm. onion, chopped

1 c. celery, chopped
1 (2 1/2 to 3-lb.) fryer chicken, cut up
1 env. dry onion soup

Mix first 5 ingredients together in greased baking dish. Place chicken on top of mixture. Sprinkle dry onion soup on top. Cover with lid and bake at 350° for 1 to 1 1/2 hours or until well done. The last 15 minutes, remove cover and let brown. (I use chicken thighs most of the time.) Serves 6.

Marge Todd

23304-98

PICK UP CHICKEN STICKS

3 lbs. chicken wings
1½ c. flour
⅓ c. sesame seeds

1 c. melted butter
1 T. salt
½ tsp. ground ginger

Cut off and discard wing tips. Divide wings in half. Wash and drain on paper towel. Melt butter. Mix flour, seeds, salt and ginger in pie plate. Roll chicken pieces, one at a time, in butter, letting excess drip back. Roll in flour mixture, then set aside until all are coated. Put in single layer in same pan. Bake in 350° oven for 1 hour or until tender. Slide pan in heated broiler for 5 minutes.

Joan Pharis

PORTED GAME HEMS

6 Rock Cornish game hens
About 4½ c. wild rice stuffing
2 T. butter or margarine
4 whole cloves
½ c. California Port

Butter or margarine
½ c. currant jelly
Juice of ½ lemon
Dash salt

Stuff each game hen with about ¾ cup wild rice dressing. Rub hens with butter. In a saucepan, combine jelly, 2 tablespoons butter, lemon juice, cloves and salt. Bring to boiling and simmer 5 minutes. Remove from heat; add the Port. Roast hens in very hot oven (450°) for 10 minutes. Reduce heat to 350° and continue cooking for 1½ hours, basting with wine sauce. If desired, just before removing birds from oven, brown under broiler for a minute or two. Asparagus and spiced crabapples are a colorful and appropriate accompaniment. Include a Caesar salad, hot rolls and frozen lime pie for dessert. Mrs. Burton's choice of wine to accompany this dish: California Grey Riesling.

Variation: Split the game hens in half and do not stuff them. Serves 4 to 6.

Carolyn Walter
Mrs. A. H. Burton, Roma Wine Co., Fresno

RASPBERRY CHICKEN

4 (4-oz.) chicken breasts,
  boneless & skinned
½ jar raspberry spread (no sugar)
½ c. pineapple juice (no sugar)
½ c. soy sauce
2 T. rice vinegar

½ tsp. chili powder
½ tsp. curry powder
½ tsp. garlic powder
½ c. fresh raspberries, mashed (¼
  for sauce)
½ c. fresh basil

Mix all ingredients except for ¼ cup sauce. Marinate several hours or overnight. Bake 30 minutes at 350°. Use the other ¼ cup fresh berries for garnish.

Joan Pharis

SOUTHWEST ROLL-UPS

2 T. salsa
1 to 2 jalapeño peppers, seeded
1 garlic clove
2 T. chopped onion
1 (16-oz.) can refried beans
½ tsp. ground cumin
1 T. chopped fresh cilantro (opt.)

1 c. cubed cooked chicken
1 c. (4 oz.) shredded cheddar
  cheese, divided
10 to 12 (6-inch) flour tortillas
Sour cream & additional salsa
  (opt.)

Place the first 8 ingredients and ½ cup cheese in a food processor. Blend until smooth. Spread evenly over tortillas. Roll up and place, seam side down, in a greased 13 x 9 x 2-inch baking dish. Cover and bake at 350° for 20 minutes or until heated through. Sprinkle with remaining cheese. Let stand until cheese melts. Serve with sour cream and salsa, if desired. Yields 10 to 12 servings.

Erma Donaldson

STIR-FRY CHICKEN

2 cans cream of celery soup
⅓ c. mayonnaise
2 tsp. paprika
2 whole chicken breasts, split,
  skinned & boned

2 c. sliced veggies (celery, onion,
  green pepper)
1 zucchini (I use more)
Hot cooked rice

In skillet blend first 3 ingredients. Stir in veggies and chicken. Over medium heat, heat to boiling. Reduce heat to low. Cover and simmer 20 minutes, until chicken is tender, stirring occasionally. Serve over hot rice. Serves 4.

Marge Todd

TURKEY OR CHICKEN HASH

1 sm. onion
2 T. dry chicken bouillon
1½ T. flour
1½ c. cubed boiled potatoes
1 T. chopped parsley
1½ c. diced cooked turkey or
  chicken

¼ c. chopped celery
2 T. oil
1 c. skim milk
Salt to taste
Pepper to taste

Sauté onion and celery in oil until limp. Dissolve bouillon and flour in skim milk. Combine with potatoes, turkey and parsley. Add salt and pepper to taste. Add to onion and celery and cook over low heat until some of the moisture has been absorbed. Turn hash over with a spatula to brown well on both sides.

Joan Pharis

23304-98

Soups,
Salads
&
Vegetables

Helpful Hints

• Fresh lemon juice will remove onion scent from hands.

• To save money and vitamins: Pour all leftover vegetables and water they are cooked in, into a freezer container. When full, add tomato juice, seasoning and have "free" soup for lunch.

• Three large stalks of cut-up celery added to about two cups of beans (navy, brown, pinto, etc.) will make them more easily digested, as will a bit of soda.

• When cooking vegetables that grow above ground, remember to boil them without a cover.

• Allow 1/4 teaspoon salt to each cup of water for cooking vegetables.

• A lump of sugar added to water when cooking vegetable greens helps retain their fresh color.

• Never soak vegetables after slicing; you will lose much of their nutritional value.

• Fresh vegetables require little seasoning or cooking. If the vegetable is old, dress it up with sauces or seasoning.

• To bake potatoes quickly, place them in boiling water for 10-15 minutes. Pierce skin with a fork and then bake in a preheated oven.

• To cut down on odors when cooking cabbage, cauliflower, etc., add a little vinegar to the cooking water.

• To avoid tears when cutting onions, try cutting them under cold running water or placing them in the freezer briefly before cutting.

• A little vinegar or lemon juice added to potatoes before draining will make them extra white when mashed.

• To avoid toughening beans or corn, add salt when cooking is halfway through.

• To dress up buttered, cooked vegetables, sprinkle them with toasted sesame seed, toasted chopped nuts, crumbled cooked bacon, canned french-fried onions, or slightly crushed seasoned croutons.

• When you're grilling your main dish, try grilling your vegetables, too, for an easy no-mess side dish.

SOUPS, SALADS & VEGETABLES

ALBONDIGAS SOUP

8 c. water
8 tsp. beef bouillon, dried
2 lg. onions, chopped
1 lb. ground beef, extra lean
1/3 c. wheat germ, toasted
1 cabbage head, chopped

16 oz. tomato sauce
4 cloves garlic
1/4 c. brown rice
Dash salt
Carrots, sliced
1 egg

Combine water, bouillon, tomato sauce, garlic and onion in large pot and heat to boiling. Meanwhile, combine remaining ingredients except carrots and cabbage. Once liquid is boiling, carefully drop in 1-inch balls of meat mixture, one at a time, forming them as you go. When all the balls are in, add vegetables. Reduce heat and cook soup until vegetables are cooked. You can tell when the meatballs are cooked because they float back up to the surface of the soup. You can substitute or add any vegetables you have on hand.

Cindi Rogers

CHICKEN NOODLE SOUP

4 med.-sized leeks (white part only)
8 c. water
2 T. cider vinegar
1 c. unsalted butter
2 med. carrots, peeled, finely chopped
2 tsp. coarse salt (kosher)
3 ribs celery, finely chopped
1 c. dry white wine
1 tsp. freshly ground black pepper

2 1/2 qt. homemade chicken stock OR canned chicken soup
2 whole chicken breasts, skinned & boned
8 med. mushrooms, wiped clean and thinly sliced
2 c. cooked thin egg noodles
4 oz. green beans, ends trimmed, diagonally sliced
3 T. chopped fresh Italian parsley

Cut the leeks lengthwise in half and soak in water mixed with the vinegar for 15 minutes. Drain and rinse the leeks. Cut into fine dice. Melt the butter in a large heavy saucepan over medium-low heat. Add the leeks, carrots, celery, salt and pepper. Cook gently for 5 minutes. Remove from heat. Heat the chicken stock and wine in a second large saucepan to boiling. Add the chicken. Reduce heat and simmer, uncovered, for 15 minutes. Remove the chicken and let cool. Add the stock and mushrooms to the vegetables. Simmer, uncovered, over low heat for 10 minutes. Add the noodles and green beans. Simmer for another 5 minutes. Remove from heat. Shred the chicken breasts and add to the soup. Add the chopped parsley and stir well. Serve immediately.

Linda Dungan

CREAM OF ZUCCHINI SOUP

1 lg. onion, chopped
3 c. chicken stock
3 stalks celery, chopped fine
6 med. zucchini, sliced 1/4 inch thick

1 can evaporated skim milk
1/4 c. oil
1 c. white wine
Dash thyme
Salt & pepper to taste

(continued)

Sauté onion and celery in oil until soft and golden. Add the stock, wine, zucchini, few celery leaves and a dash of thyme. Simmer until the zucchini is soft. Purée. Add evaporated milk and salt and pepper to taste.

Cindi Rogers

LIMA BEAN CHOWDER

1 c. lima beans
1 c. diced potatoes
½ lb. bacon, cut into cubes
4 c. milk

3 c. water
1 onion, chopped
1 T. flour

Cook lima beans in water until tender. Cook diced potatoes until tender. Fry bacon. Brown onion in bacon fat. Drain fat and reserve. Add lima beans and potatoes to onion and bacon. In 1 tablespoon bacon fat, stir in 1 tablespoon flour and add 4 cups milk. Cook until smooth. Add to lima beans and serve hot.

Jean Edwards

POTATO & ONION SOUP

(Minestrina Di Patate)

It is best **not** to substitute the freshly grated cheese with the canned variety.

2 lbs. potatoes, roughly cut
1 lg. onion, chopped
¼ c. carrots, finely chopped
¼ c. celery, finely chopped
½ c. oil

½ c. Parmesan cheese, freshly
 grated
2 cans evaporated skim milk
2 cans chicken broth, condensed

Cook potatoes in just enough water with chicken broth added to cover until tender. Mash potatoes in pot with cooking liquid. In fry pan, sauté onion, carrot and celery in oil until onion is clear and vegetables are still slightly crunchy; add to potatoes. Add Parmesan cheese and sufficient milk for desired consistency to potatoes; bring to slow boil. Lower heat and cook for 2 to 3 minutes, **stirring constantly**. Serve with additional grated cheese on top.

Cindi Rogers

SALMON CHOWDER

1 sm. onion, thinly sliced
1 can cream of celery soup
1 can salmon, drained
1 T. minced parsley, for garnish

1 T. butter
1⅓ c. milk
1 can creamed corn

In a large saucepan, sauté onion in butter until tender. Stir in remaining ingredients and heat through. This was originally in Country Woman's Magazine. Delicious!

Marge Todd

23304-98

PUMPKIN STEW

2 lbs. stew meat, cut into 1-inch
  cubes
1 c. water
3 T. cooking oil, divided
4 med. carrots, sliced
3 lg. potatoes, peeled & cut into
  1-inch cubes
4 garlic cloves, minced
1 lg. green pepper, cut into ½-inch
  pieces

1 med. onion, chopped
2 tsp. salt
½ tsp. pepper
2 T. instant beef bouillon granules
1 (10 to 12-lb.) pumpkin
1 (14½-oz.) can tomatoes,
  undrained, cut up

In a Dutch oven, brown meat in 2 tablespoons oil. Add water, potatoes, carrots, green pepper, garlic, onion, salt and pepper. Cover and simmer for 2 hours. Stir in bouillon and tomatoes. Wash pumpkin and cut a 6 to 8-inch circle around top stem. Remove top and set aside; discard seeds and loose fibers from inside. Place pumpkin in a shallow sturdy baking pan. Spoon stew into pumpkin and replace the top. Brush outside of pumpkin with remaining oil. Bake at 325° for 2 hours or just until the pumpkin is tender (do not overbake). Serve stew from pumpkin, scooping out a little pumpkin with each serving.

Erma Donaldson

TACO SOUP

(Easy)

1 c. chopped onion
2 c. water
1 can diced chilies
2 cans red kidney beans

2 can whole tomatoes, chopped
2 cans tomato sauce
½ lb. ground beef
1 env. taco seasoning

Combine ingredients and simmer for 20 minutes. Serve with plain yogurt or sour cream, shredded cheese and corn chips.

Joan Pharis

TACO SOUP

1½ lbs. ground beef
1 (28-oz.) can tomatoes with juice
1 (14-oz.) can kidney beans with
  juice
1 to 2 c. water, as needed
1 (17-oz.) can corn with juice

1 c. grated cheddar cheese
½ c. chopped onion
1 pkg. taco seasoning
Dash salt
Dash pepper

Brown beef in large heavy kettle. Drain. Add onions and cook until tender. Add remaining ingredients (except cheese) and simmer 15 minutes. Ladle into bowls. Top with grated cheese. Serve with taco chips.

Marge Todd

ZUCCHINI SOUP

3 lbs. zucchini, cut into chunks
1 onion, cut up
4 beef bouillon cubes
3 T. parsley
Pepper to taste

4 strips bacon
1 qt. water
1 T. sweet basil
Salt to taste

Cook in large pot for 30 minutes. Put through blender. Serve hot.

Joan Pharis

4-BEAN SALAD

1 can red beans
1 can yellow beans
1 c. chopped onion
¾ c. chopped pepper
½ c. vinegar
Dash pepper

1 can green beans
1 can garbanzo beans
½ c. salad oil
¾ c. sugar
1 tsp. salt

Mix all ingredients; refrigerate overnight. Serve the following day.

Ruth Caudill

4-BEAN SALAD

Dressing:

½ c. sugar
⅔ c. vinegar
½ tsp. Worcestershire sauce

½ c. salad oil
½ tsp. salt (opt.)
⅓ tsp. pepper

Drain:

1 can Blue Lake green beans, cut
1 can wax beans

1 can kidney beans
1 can garbanzo beans (opt.)

Cut up:

1 green pepper, slivered, cut bite-sized
1 red onion, sliced thin & then cut bite-sized

1 can sm. olives

Mix dressing well in a large bowl. Add remaining ingredients. Let stand overnight in refrigerator. Dressing will keep for several days. Makes about 8 cups dressing.

Susan Fiske

BEET SALAD

1 (6-oz.) pkg. raspberry Jello
1 (No. 2) can crushed pineapple

1 (No. 2) can STRING beets
¼ c. vinegar

(continued)

23304-98

Dissolve Jello in 2 cups boiling water. Add 1¼ cups pineapple juice and the ¼ cup vinegar, then add the drained pineapple and beets. Chill. Serves 12.

Fran Delano

CABBAGE-CHICKEN SALAD

2 T. sugar
6 T. red wine vinegar
2 to 4 green onions, sliced
2 pkgs. ramen noodles, broken
1 whole chicken breast, cooked &
  cubed

½ c. oil
½ tsp. pepper
½ tsp. salt

Mix all ingredients together. Marinate overnight. Toss with 1 head sliced cabbage and 2 tablespoons toasted sesame seeds. **Optional:** Instead of sesame seeds, use 2 to 4 tablespoons sliced almonds or sunflower seeds.

Alice Fritz Gerber

CATALINA SPINACH SALAD

½ c. vegetable oil
¼ c. red wine vinegar
¼ c. finely chopped onion
2 tsp. Worcestershire sauce
2 (10-oz.) bags spinach, torn
2 (8-oz.) cans sliced water
  chestnuts, drained
2 c. chow mein noodles

2 hard-cooked eggs, chopped
12 bacon strips, cooked &
  crumbled
¼ c. ketchup
3 T. sugar
½ tsp. salt
2 lg. tomatoes, diced

Combine the oil, ketchup, wine vinegar, onion, sugar, Worcestershire sauce and salt in a jar with tight-fitting lid. Shake well. Combine remaining ingredients in a large salad bowl. Add dressing and toss. Serve immediately. Yields 6 to 8 servings.

Erma Donaldson

CHESTNUTS & PEAS SALAD

1 pkg. frozen green petite peas,
  uncooked
1 c. celery
1 c. water chestnuts, sliced

½ c. green onions, chopped
1 c. mayonnaise
Lemon pepper to taste

Combine all ingredients and refrigerate long enough for peas to be completely thawed.

Mildred Walters

CHICKEN (OR HAM) MACARONI SALAD
(Filipino-Style)

1 lb. salad macaroni, cooked & drained
4 chicken breasts, halved & cooked & diced
1 sm. can pineapple chunks, cut in half
2 apples, pared, cored & diced
2 stalks celery, diced
½ c. cooked diced carrots
½ c. diced mild cheddar cheese
½ c. raisins
2 T. sweet pickle relish
1 can sweetened condensed milk
1 qt. (32 oz.) mayonnaise
Dash pepper

Combine all ingredients and mix until all is well coated with mayonnaise. Refrigerate overnight. Ham can be used in place of chicken (1 pound ham slices, chopped).

Basil Anderson

COLESLAW

1 firm head cabbage, chopped
1 green pepper, chopped
6 green onions, chopped
½ c. sugar
1 c. white vinegar
3 carrots, grated
1 tsp. salt
2 tsp. celery seed
⅔ c. oil
2 tsp. dry mustard

Mix vegetables together. Add sugar and salt. Mix white vinegar, celery seed and mustard. Bring to a boil and add oil. Stir well and pour over vegetables immediately. This keeps well for several days.

Judy Burtoft

COLESLAW DRESSING

½ c. mayonnaise OR ½ c. low-fat mayonnaise
¼ c. sugar OR 6 pkgs. Equal
2 T. vinegar OR 1 T. vinegar

Susan Fiske

CORN SALAD

Dressing:

¼ c. oil
3 T. lime juice (approx. 1 lime)
2 T. chopped fresh parsley
1 tsp. chili powder
½ tsp. coriander
½ tsp. hot paprika
½ tsp. oregano
¼ tsp. salt

Whisk dressing together and pour over:

1½ c. black olives, halved
16 oz. frozen corn, thawed
1 red bell pepper, diced
1 green bell pepper, diced
1½ c. grated cheddar cheese
½ c. canned garbanzo beans, drained
4 green onions, sliced

(continued)

23304-98

Stir well. This is best made a few hours before serving.

Alice Fritz Gerber

CORNED BEEF SALAD

1 can corned beef
1½ c. celery, cut fine
1 slice onion
2 pkgs. Knox gelatin
⅓ green pepper
1½ c. mayonnaise (or Miracle
  Whip)

Pickles (garnish)
Eggs (garnish)
Olives (garnish)
2 c. cooked macaroni (opt.)

Dissolve the packages of gelatin in a cup of cold water first, then a cup of boiling water. When cool, stir gradually into mayonnaise and mix thoroughly. Put everything else except celery through food grinder (medium blade) and add to the gelatin, stirring it in. Mold and garnish with eggs, olives, pickles, etc. Can be stretched by adding 2 cups cooked macaroni to cooled mixture. Serves 8 to 10 and is best made ahead.

Eleanor Fritz

CRAB-PASTA SALAD

While pasta cooks, prepare dressing and vegetables.

Dressing (whisk together in a lg. bowl):

3 T. vinegar
1 T. Dijon mustard
Pepper to taste

¼ c. olive oil
½ tsp. tarragon
Salt (opt.)

Salad (add to dressing - mix to coat all):

2 c. (6 oz.) corkscrew pasta (or any shape), cooked & drained
8 oz. (or more) crab meat, cut bite-sized
½ green, red or gold pepper (or combo), sliced thin & cut bite-sized

½ red onion, chopped
1 c. sm. olives

Decorate with spinach, lettuce or parsley. Keeps in refrigerator for several days. Makes about 7 cups.

Susan Fiske

CRANBERRY JELLO SALAD
(Thanksgiving Salad)

1 pkg. raspberry Jello
1¼ c. boiling water
1 chopped apple
1 can crushed pineapple
1 can whole cranberries

1 c. chopped celery
1 pkg. cranberry Jello
¼ c. orange juice
1 c. chopped nuts

Mix together and pour into a 9 x 13-inch loaf pan. Chill and serve. Usually cut into 15 servings. This has been used by members of Foothill Community Presbyterian Church for many years. A real favorite!

Members of FCPC

CRUNCHY PEA SALAD

Mix together:

½ c. mayonnaise

¼ c. Italian dressing

Add:

1 (10-oz.) pkg. frozen peas, thawed, drained
1 c. chopped celery
1 c. walnuts

6 crisply cooked bacon slices, crumbled
¼ c. chopped red onions

Toss and serve.

Variation: Use ham instead of bacon, green onion and bell pepper.

Joyce O'Neal

FESTIVE CORNBREAD SALAD

5 c. cubed cornbread OR 6 cornbread muffins
3 c. diced fresh tomatoes
1 c. diced sweet onion
1 c. diced green pepper
1 lb. sliced bacon, cooked & crumbled

¼ c. sweet pickle relish
1 c. mayonnaise
¼ c. sweet pickle juice
Shredded Parmesan cheese

Place cornbread cubes in a large salad bowl (or crumble muffins into bowl). Combine tomatoes, onion, green pepper, bacon and relish. Add to cornbread. Combine mayonnaise and pickle juice; mix well. Pour over vegetables. Sprinkle with Parmesan cheese. Chill until ready to serve. Serves 10 to 12.

Erma Donaldson

23304-98

FRESH BROCCOLI-MANDARIN SALAD

1 egg + 1 egg yolk, lightly beaten
1½ tsp. cornstarch
¼ c. tarragon vinegar
3 T. butter
4 c. broccoli
6 slices bacon, cooked & crumbled
2 c. sliced mushrooms
½ c. slivered almonds, toasted
½ c. red onion, sliced
1 can mandarin oranges, drained
½ c. sugar
1 tsp. dry mustard
¼ c. water
½ c. mayonnaise
½ c. raisins

In top of double boiler, whisk together egg, yolk, sugar, cornstarch and mustard. Combine vinegar and water. Pour into egg mixture, whisking constantly. Place over hot water and cook, stirring, until thickened. Remove from heat. Stir in butter and mayonnaise. Chill. Toss with remaining ingredients.

Joan Pharis

FROZEN PEA & PEANUT SALAD

1 pkg. frozen peas
4 green onions, sliced
Ranch dressing
2 c. celery, thinly sliced
1 c. Spanish peanuts

Mix peas, celery and onion. Just before serving, add dressing and peanuts.

Joan Pharis

FRENCH DRESSING

1 c. cooking oil
¼ c. vinegar
1 T. Worcestershire sauce
½ tsp. paprika
¼ c. catsup
3 T. sugar
1 tsp. garlic

Put in a jar with tight lid and shake well.

Fran Delano

FRUIT SALAD DRESSING

½ c. sugar
1 tsp. salt
1 c. salad oil
1 tsp. dry mustard
⅓ c. vinegar
1½ tsp. grated onion

Mix sugar, mustard and vinegar together. Add oil, a little at a time, using beater. Beat well. Add grated onion and mix.

Fran Delano

FRUIT SALAD DRESSING

½ c. sugar or 8 pkgs. Equal
1 tsp. dry mustard
1 c. canola
⅓ c. vinegar
½ tsp. salt
½ tsp. grated onion

(continued)

Put all ingredients in a blender and drizzle oil in slowly as it is running until it is well blended and slightly thickened. This is delicious on mixed citrus chunks or any fruit salad!

Jean Edwards

GUACAMOLE SALAD

1 head iceberg lettuce
¼ c. grated cheddar cheese
¼ c. grated Monterey Jack cheese
½ c. scallions (opt.)

8 cherry tomatoes, halved
1 c. crushed corn chips (chili cheese Fritos recommended)

Dressing:

1 avocado, peeled, pitted & mashed
1 T. fresh lemon juice
½ c. sour cream

⅓ c. corn oil
1 T. picante sauce

Tear up lettuce and combine with cheeses, scallions and tomatoes. Toss salad with dressing. Sprinkle with chips.

Marguerite McClure

HOT CHICKEN SALAD

5 chicken breasts (or 1 whole chicken), cooked, skinned & cubed
2 c. chopped celery
4 T. chopped onion
1 c. blanched almonds

3 c. cooked rice (not Minute Rice)
2 cans cream of chicken soup
1½ c. mayonnaise
6 hard-boiled eggs
1 sm. jar pimento

Topping:

1½ c. crushed BBQ potato chips

½ lb. grated cheddar cheese

Mix cubed chicken, celery, onion, almonds, rice, soup, pimento, chopped eggs and mayonnaise. Pour into greased Pyrex 9 x 13-inch dish. Cover with grated cheese and sprinkle on crushed chips. Bake at 350° for 30 minutes.

Joyce O'Neal

HOT CHICKEN SALAD

2 c. diced cooked chicken breasts
1½ c. sliced celery
½ c. sliced almonds
2 T. minced onion

2 T. lemon juice
½ tsp. salt
¼ tsp. pepper
¾ c. mayonnaise

Topping:

¾ c. grated sharp cheddar cheese

1 c. crushed potato chips

(continued)

23304-98

Combine ingredients. Place in 8 x 8-inch casserole. Spread with cheese and potato chip topping. Bake 15 minutes at 400°.

Mildred Walters

HOT HAM SALAD

1 jar pimentos	1 c. chopped water chestnuts
½ tsp. salt	½ c. mayonnaise
3 (12 oz.) Hormel smoked ham	1 T. lemon juice
2 c. chopped celery	2 tsp. grated onion

Topping:

½ c. grated Swiss cheese	1 c. crushed potato chips

Mix all ingredients together and top with cheese and potato chips. Bake at 450° for 15 minutes.

Alice Anderson

JICAMA SALAD

1 med. jicama, peeled	2 tsp. chopped unsalted peanuts
2 oranges, peeled & salted	½ tsp. crushed dried red chilies
1 tsp. chili powder	Lettuce

Cut jicama into bite-sized pieces and place in large bowl. Section oranges and cut into bite-sized pieces, holding sections over bowl so juices will fall into it. Season to taste with salt. Add chili powder, peanuts and crushed chilies. Mix well. Chill and serve on lettuce leaves. Yields 6 to 8 servings.

Joan Pharis

LEMON JELLO SALAD

6-oz. pkg. lemon Jello	3 bananas, quartered
1 sm. can crushed pineapple, drained, juice reserved	1 c. sm. marshmallows

Mix Jello per directions and chill until nearly set. Add other ingredients and chill until set. **Topping:** To the pineapple juice add enough water to make 1 cup of liquid. Mix 2 tablespoons flour with ½ cup sugar and add to juice gradually. Beat 1 egg slightly. Add to mixture and cook until thickened, stirring constantly. Remove from heat and cool. Whip the ½ cup whipping cream (not too stiff) and fold into cooked mixture. Spread topping on top of Jello and sprinkle with chopped walnuts. This is best made a day ahead. Keep refrigerated.

Dorothy Anderson

LIME JELLO-COTTAGE CHEESE SALAD

3-oz. box lime Jello	1 tall can crushed pineapple, drained
1 c. boiling water	
1 can Eagle Brand condensed milk	2 c. (1 pt.) sm. curd cottage cheese

(continued)

Mix lime Jello and boiling water to dissolve. Add condensed milk and blend. Add drained pineapple and cottage cheese. Put into dish and chill until set. Fits 8-inch square dish. Double recipe for 9 x 12-inch size.

Dorothy Anderson
Emma Green's Recipe from the 40's

LIME JELLO-PINEAPPLE-CREAM CHEESE SALAD

15 lg. marshmallows
1 pkg. lime Jello
2 (3-oz.) pkgs. cream cheese
1 (No. 2) can crushed pineapple, undrained

1 c. whipping cream, whipped
1 c. milk
2/3 c. mayonnaise
1 extra pkg. lime Jello for topping

Melt marshmallows in milk. Pour over Jello and dissolve. Add cream cheese and dissolve. Add pineapple and allow to cool. Blend in mayonnaise and whipped cream. Refrigerate until firm. Serve as is or top with 1 package lime Jello prepared according to directions, then chill until firm. Pretty!

Dorothy Anderson

MACARONI SALAD

1 lb. salad macaroni noodles, cooked as directed on pkg.
1/2 chopped ham (I use turkey ham slices, diced)
1 lb. cheddar cheese, chopped
1 (16 oz.) pineapple tidbits

3 apples, chopped
2 pieces celery, chopped
1/2 c. raisins
1 qt. mayonnaise
1 can sweetened condensed milk

Mix mayonnaise and condensed milk together. Pour over rest of the ingredients.

Marge Todd
From Basil Anderson Kitchen

ORANGE-SOUR CREAM JELLO SALAD

1 sm. pkg. lemon Jello
1 sm. pkg. orange Jello
1 sm. can mandarin oranges
1 sm. ctn. sour cream

1 1/4 c. grated mild cheddar cheese
2 c. mini marshmallows
1 can pineapple tidbits
1/4 c. mayonnaise

Combine dry Jello in large bowl. Drain pineapple and oranges, saving the juice. Add 2 cups boiling water to Jello. Add enough cold water to the fruit juices to make 2 cups and add that to the Jello. Refrigerate until slightly set. Stir in the fruit and marshmallows. Return to refrigerator and chill until set completely. Add 1/3 cup mayonnaise to sour cream and spread over Jello. Top with the grated cheese.

Dorothy Anderson

23304-98

PACIFIC LIME MOLD

1 c. boiling water
1 tsp. horseradish
9-oz. can crushed pineapple,
  drained, juice reserved
1 c. creamy cottage cheese
½ c. mayonnaise, whipped
3-oz. pkg. lime Jello
¼ c. chopped nuts

Dissolve gelatin in water. Add juice from pineapple. Chill until slightly thickened. Beat until frothy. Fold in remaining ingredients. Chill until set.

Marge Lowery

PISTACHIO-COOL WHIP SALAD

1 lg. tub Cool Whip
1 sm. pkg. dry instant pistachio
  pudding
1 can crushed pineapple, undrained
1 c. miniature marshmallows
1 handful chopped nuts, if desired

Combine and chill. Best if made a day ahead.

Dorothy Anderson

QUICK JELLO SALAD

1 pt. cottage cheese
1 lg. ctn. Cool Whip
1 pkg. lime Jello, dry (or other
  flavor)
1 can crushed pineapple, drained

Mix together and put in serving bowl. Sprinkle with chopped nuts. Chill and serve. This is almost ready to be served immediately.

Betty Baird

RECEPTION SALAD

1 lg. pkg. lemon gelatin
1 lg. can crushed pineapple,
  drained & juice saved
2 sm. pkgs. cream cheese
1 can chopped pimiento
½ c. celery, cut finely
2 c. (1 env.) Dream Whip, prepared

Mash cream cheese with chopped pimiento. Heat pineapple juice and add gelatin. When it begins to gel, add other ingredients and pour into large dish. Chill.

Elaine Straube

RICE SALAD

1 pkg. chicken Rice-A-Roni
2 jars marinated artichokes,
  drained, juice from 1 jar saved
1 sm. can mushrooms
1 can sliced olives
1 can water chestnuts
1 can meat (chicken, crab or
  shrimp - opt.)
¾ c. mayonnaise

(continued)

Prepare rice as directed on the package. Mix artichoke juice and mayonnaise. Add to prepared rice. Mix remaining ingredients. Chill and serve cold.

Kathie Gifford

SOUR CREAM-FRUIT SALAD

1 qt. canned pears in pieces,
 drained
1-qt. can chunk-style pineapple

2 c. seedless grapes, halved
1 c. shredded coconut
1 pt. sour cream

Mix and let stand in the refrigerator for several hours, stirring often.

Dorothy Anderson

SPICED PEACH SALAD

1 (1-lb. size) can sliced cling
 peaches
1/4 c. vinegar
20 whole cloves

1 (3-oz.) pkg. orange Jello
1/2 c. sugar
1/3 tsp. cinnamon
3/4 c. cold water

Drain peaches, reserving 3/4 cup of syrup. Chop peaches coarsely. Bring syrup, vinegar, sugar and spices to boil. Add peaches and simmer 10 minutes. Strain syrup and discard cloves. Add boiling water to make 1 cup, if necessary. Dissolve Jello in hot syrup. Add cold water and peaches. Chill until set, stirring occasionally at first to distribute peaches evenly.

Dorothy Anderson

SPINACH-APPLE SALAD

2 T. cider vinegar
1/4 tsp. salt
1 c. diced unpeeled apple
1/4 c. chopped sweet onion
2 c. torn fresh spinach

2 T. vegetable oil
1/4 tsp. sugar
1/4 c. raisins
2 c. torn romaine

In a small bowl, combine vinegar, oil, salt and sugar. Mix well. Add apple, onion and raisins. Toss lightly to coat. Cover and let stand for 10 minutes. Just before serving, combine spinach and romaine in a large salad bowl. Add dressing and toss.

Erma Donaldson

STRAWBERRY-BANANA JELLO

1 lg. box strawberry Jello
2 boxes frozen sliced strawberries
3 lg. bananas, mashed

1 (No. 2 1/2) can crushed pineapple,
 drained
1 lg. ctn. sour cream

Add 2 cups boiling water to Jello in a large bowl. Add 2 boxes of frozen strawberries. Stir until berries are broken up and mixed in. Add bananas and pineapple. Pour half the mixture into an 8 x 12-inch or 9 x 13-inch dish. When firm, cover with the sour cream and pour remaining Jello on top. Chill.

Dorothy Anderson

23304-98

THOUSAND ISLAND SALAD DRESSING

2 parts mayonnaise (Best Foods)
1 part catsup
1 tsp. lemon juice
Pinch garlic, to taste

Mix together and serve.

Susan Fiske

TROPICAL CHICKEN CONDIMENT SALAD

1½ c. mayonnaise
1 c. raisins, plumped in white wine
  or water, drained
1 c. salted peanuts
1 c. mango chutney, cut if
  necessary
1 c. flaked coconut
4 to 5 c. cooked chicken meat,
  coarsely diced
2 c. sliced bananas
Salt & pepper to taste
Avocados, peeled & sliced

Blend together mayonnaise, raisins, nuts, chutney and coconut. Fold in chicken and bananas. Season and chill. To serve, line large salad bowl (or individual plates) with lettuce. Mound salad on lettuce and garnish with lemon-dipped avocado slices (and pineapple or more bananas, if desired).

Mildred Walters

TUNA SALAD
(Tuna Salad Sandwich Spread)

1 (6½-oz.) can tuna OR salmon,
  water packed, drained
¼ c. finely chopped celery
¼ c. finely chopped onion
2 T. finely chopped parsley
⅓ c. plain nonfat yogurt
½ T. honey
1 tsp. lemon juice
1 T. prepared mustard, spicy or
  Dijon

Flake fish. Add vegetables. Combine yogurt, honey, lemon juice and mustard. Mix with fish. No added fat. 159 calories. 1 gram fat (salmon/4 grams). 58 milligrams cholesterol.

Susan Fiske

VEGETABLE JELLO SALAD

1 c. boiling water
2 T. chopped olives
2 T. celery, chopped fine
2 T. onion, chopped fine (or dry)
1 sm. ctn. cottage cheese
1 (3-oz.) pkg. lime Jello
½ c. milk
½ c. mayonnaise
2 T. grated carrots

Mix Jello and boiling water to dissolve and allow to cool. Mix cottage cheese with mayonnaise and milk. Add to Jello mixture and refrigerate until almost set. Add in rest of ingredients and chill until set.

Betty Lynn

ANYTIME POTATOES

Enough potatoes for your family

Scrub potatoes with wire brush. Slice thin and layer with thin slices of onions or chopped onions. Sprinkle with McKay's chicken-like seasoning on each layer. Microwave, covered so the potatoes will steam in their own juice, until done. Serve as is or transfer to fry pan to brown (using Pam) or brown in oven. This is from a Seventh Day Adventist cooking class. No added fat or oil (light spray of Pam). Favorite potato for this is red skin, "new potatoes."

Susan Fiske

BROCCOLI HOT DISH

1 pkg. frozen chopped broccoli, cooked for ½ time on pkg.
1 c. Minute Rice, cooked
½ c. onion, chopped
½ c. celery, chopped
1 can cream of mushroom soup
1 sm. jar Cheez Whiz with pimento

Prepare all the above ingredients and combine in casserole dish. Bake at 350° for 30 minutes.

Sandy Schluter
Lutheran Church in Minnesota

CARROT MARINADE

Cut 2 pounds carrots in diagonal slices. Cook in a little water (or steam) until tender. Drain if water is used. Blend the following in saucepan and simmer for 5 minutes:

1 can Campbell's tomato soup
1 tsp. Worcestershire sauce
1 tsp. prepared mustard
1 c. sugar
½ c. vinegar
½ c. Mazola or other oil

Pour over carrots. Add ½ cup each chopped onion and bell pepper. Stir to mix and refrigerate. Use less sauce for less spicy carrots. Marinate at least 24 hours.

Dorothy Anderson

COPPER PENNIES

2 lbs. carrots, peeled, sliced round
2 med. onions, sliced thin
1 bell pepper, sliced thin
1 (10-oz.) can tomato soup
¾ c. vinegar
1 tsp. Lea & Perrins Worcestershire sauce
1 tsp. prepared mustard
½ tsp. salt
½ tsp. pepper
4 ribs celery, sliced thin

Cook carrots until tender but firm; drain and set aside. Combine soup, vinegar, a little sugar, Worcestershire sauce, mustard, salt, pepper, onion, bell pepper and celery. Heat to boil; stir. Simmer less than 10 minutes. Pour over drained carrots. Serve hot or refrigerate for a salad. Serves 6 to 8.

Margaret Baird

23304-98

KEN'S SWEET POTATOES

8 med. sweet potatoes
1¼ c. packed brown sugar
½ c. apple juice

¼ c. butter or margarine
½ c. raisins
½ c. water

Cook and peel potatoes and allow to cool. Slice and place in a greased 2½-quart baking dish. In a small saucepan, combine remaining ingredients and bring to a boil, stirring frequently. Pour over the potatoes. Bake, uncovered, at 350° for 45 minutes, basting occasionally. Serves 8.

Erma Donaldson

MAPLE WHIPPED BUTTERNUT SQUASH

2 lbs. squash, peeled
¼ c. maple syrup
3 T. brown sugar, firmly packed
1 beaten egg

½ c. butter
¾ tsp. nutmeg
Dash salt
Dash pepper

Cook squash until tender. Drain and mash. Mix the rest of the ingredients and add to squash. Place in casserole. Bake at 350° for about 30 minutes.

Ruth Caudill

MARINATED VEGETABLES

16-oz. can Le Sueur peas (or plain peas)
12-oz. can shoe peg corn (or plain corn)
16-oz. can French-style green beans

1 chopped onion
¾ c. chopped celery
1 med. bell pepper, chopped

Combine all of the above, then heat to boiling:

½ c. salad oil
½ c. wine vinegar
¾ c. sugar

1 tsp. salt
½ tsp. pepper

Mix into vegetables. Let stand 24 hours. Keeps several weeks.

Dorothy Anderson

MASHED SWEET POTATOES BAKED

¼ c. margarine
1 tsp. cinnamon
6 med. sweet potatoes, cooked & mashed or 1-lb. 13-oz. can sweet potatoes, mashed

2 c. miniature marshmallows
½ c. milk
¼ tsp. salt

Add margarine, milk, cinnamon and salt to mashed potatoes. Beat until smooth, light and fluffy. Spoon into greased 1½-quart casserole. Cover with marshmallows.

(continued)

Bake, uncovered, at 350° for 20 to 30 minutes or until heated through and marsh-mallows are lightly browned. Serves 6 to 8.

Marge Lowery

SKILLED CREAMED POTATOES

6 med. potatoes, boiled & diced
2 c. sour cream
2 T. pimiento-stuffed olives,
  chopped fine
3 T. chopped onion

1 tsp. salt
½ tsp. pepper
½ tsp. paprika
1 T. chopped parsley

Cook and dice potatoes; reverse. Pour sour cream into skillet and add potatoes. Heat slowly until sour cream is bubbly. Add onions, olives, salt and pepper. Heat through. Garnish with paprika and parsley. This was enjoyed at Peggy Todd's.

Dorothy Anderson

SWEET POTATO BALLS

2½ c. mashed sweet potatoes
½ tsp. salt
⅓ c. honey
2 T. melted butter

10 marshmallows
1 c. chopped pecans
Dash pepper
1 T. butter

Combine potatoes, salt, pepper and 2 tablespoons melted butter. Chill for easy handling. Shape in balls with marshmallow in center of each. (I use size of ice cream scoop.) Heat honey and 1 tablespoon butter in small pan. Let cool slightly, then coat each ball in glaze. Roll in chopped nuts. Space balls so they do not touch in greased shallow baking dish. Bake in 350° oven for 20 to 25 minutes.

Mildred Walters

Recipe Favorites

23304-98

This &
That

Helpful Hints

• Refinish Antiques or Revitalize Wood: Use equal parts of linseed oil, white vinegar, and turpentine. Rub into furniture (or wood) with soft cloth and lots of elbow grease.

• Stalk the ants in your pantry and seal off cracks where they are entering with putty or petroleum jelly. Try sprinkling red pepper on floors and counter tops.

• For ease in sliding, rub wax along sliding doors, windows and wooden drawers that stick.

• A simple polish for copper bottom cookware: equal portions of flour and salt made into a paste with vinegar. Keep in refrigerator.

• Iron cleaner: Baking soda on a damp sponge will remove starch deposits. Make sure the iron is cold and unplugged.

• Remove stale odors in the wash by adding baking soda.

• To clean Teflon: Combine 1 cup water, 2 tablespoons baking soda, 1/2 cup liquid bleach and boil in stained pan for 5-10 minutes or until stain disappears. Wash, rinse and dry, and condition with oil before using pan again.

• Corningware cookware can be cleaned by filling them with water and dropping in two denture cleaning tablets. Let stand for 30-45 minutes.

• A little instant coffee will work wonders on your furniture. Just make a thick paste of your favorite instant and a little water, and rub it into the nicks and scratches on your dark wood furniture. You'll be overjoyed at how new and beautiful those pieces will look.

• For clogged shower head, try boiling it in 1/2 cup vinegar and 1 quart water for 15 minutes.

• For a spicy aroma, toss dried orange and lemon rinds into your fireplace.

• Tin coffee cans make excellent freezer containers for cookies.

• Add raw rice to the salt shaker to keep the salt free-flowing.

• Ice cubes will help sharpen the garbage disposer blades.

• Vinegar will remove rust and mildew stains from most chrome.

THIS & THAT

MINTED NUTS

1 c. sugar
½ c. water
1 T. light corn syrup
½ tsp. essence of peppermint or 3
  drops oil of peppermint

6 marshmallows
⅛ tsp. salt
1 c. walnuts

Cook together slowly: sugar, water, corn syrup and salt. Remove from heat just before it forms a soft ball stage when a little is dropped in cold water or 230° on candy thermometer. Add marshmallows. Stir until marshmallows are melted. Add peppermint and nuts and stir with circular motion until every nut is coated and mixture hardens. Cool on unglazed paper. These can be kept fresh in tightly covered jar for some weeks.

Mildred Walters

MICROWAVED SUGAR-GLAZED WALNUTS

⅓ c. butter or margarine
1 c. brown sugar, packed
1 lg. walnut halves or lg. pieces
  (about 4 c.)

1 tsp. cinnamon

In 1½-quart casserole, place butter. Microwave at high 1 minute or until melted. Stir in brown sugar and cinnamon. Microwave at high 2 minutes. Mix well to combine butter and sugar. Add nuts and mix to coat. Microwave at high about 4 to 5 minutes. Spread out onto waxed paper and cool. Makes about 1 pound.

Marge Lowery

SUGARED NUTS

½ c. sugar
4 T. water
2 c. nuts (she used walnuts)

½ c. brown sugar
Pinch salt
A little cinnamon

Boil sugars, water, salt and cinnamon until it spins a long thread. Add nuts. Stir with fork until all are coated. Cool.

Millie Baird
Christmas, 1940

CRANBERRY-ORANGE RELISH

2 lbs. fresh or frozen cranberries (8
  c.)
2 c. water

1 c. packed brown sugar
1 c. golden raisins
2 oranges, peeled & diced

Combine cranberries and water in a heavy saucepan. Bring to a boil, then cook over medium heat until cranberries pop, about 5 minutes. Add sugar, raisins and

(continued)

oranges. Cook over medium heat about 15 minutes or until thickened, stirring occasionally. Cool, then chill. Makes about 6 cups.

Fran Delano

SWEET DILL CHIPS
(Easy)

½ gal. sliced dill pickles, drained (Polish Vlasic), crunchy
2 lg. cloves garlic, sliced
4 c. sugar

2 c. cider vinegar
12 to 14 whole cloves
1 (3-inch) stick cinnamon
1 T. chopped pimiento (opt.)

Place pickles, garlic and pimiento (optional) in a large bowl. Combine sugar, vinegar and spices in a saucepan and bring to a boil. Simmer 10 minutes. Pour over pickles and let cool, stirring twice. When cold, remove cinnamon and cloves. Put pickles back in jar, draining liquid. Boil liquid again and pour over pickles while hot. Cool and refrigerate. Cover lightly and wait 10 days before eating.

Mildred Walters

ZUCCHINI SWEET RELISH

Grind and let stand overnight:

10 c. squash (about 6 lbs.)
4 c. onions

5 T. salt

Drain and rinse with cold water. Add:

2½ c. vinegar (full strength)
6 c. sugar
1 T. each nutmeg, dry mustard, turmeric, cornstarch

½ tsp. black pepper
2 tsp. celery seed
1 red & 1 green pepper, chopped

Cook and stir for 30 minutes. Seal with hot lids in canning jars. Makes approximately 7 pints.

Susan Fiske

WHITE SAUCE MIX

2 c. nonfat dry milk powder
1 c. flour, whole-grain wheat is okay

2 tsp. salt
1 c. margarine, still hard

Combine in food processor. Store in refrigerator. To make sauce, combine ½ cup mix with 1 cup liquid (water, milk, broth, tomato juice) in saucepan. Heat over medium until thickened.

Variations: For cheese sauce, add cheese. For curry sauce, add 1 teaspoon curry. This is good to keep on hand in the refrigerator. It is very, very easy to make and is foolproof.

Cindi Rogers

23304-98

INDEX OF RECIPES

SOUPS, SALADS & VEGETABLES

MEATS, FISH & POULTRY

THIS & THAT

How to Order

Get your additional copies of this cookbook by returning an order form and your check or money order to:

**Presbyterian Women of
Foothill Community Presbyterian Church
19752 Guthrie, P.O. Box 125
Strathmore, CA 93267
(209) 568-1771**

Please send me _____ copies of the **Seasoned with Love** cookbook at **$8.00** per copy and **$1.50** for shipping and handling per book. Enclosed is my check or money order for $_____.

Mail Books To:

Name _____

Address _____

City _____ State _____ Zip _____

Please send me _____ copies of the **Seasoned with Love** cookbook at **$8.00** per copy and **$1.50** for shipping and handling per book. Enclosed is my check or money order for $_____.

Mail Books To:

Name _____

Address _____

City _____ State _____ Zip _____

COOKING TIPS

- After stewing a chicken for diced meat for casseroles, etc., let cool in broth before cutting into chunks–it will have twice the flavor.

- To slice meat into thin strips, as for Chinese dishes–partially freeze and it will slice easily.

- A roast with the bone in will cook faster than a boneless roast–the bone carries the heat to the inside of the roast quicker.

- Never cook a roast cold–let stand for a least an hour at room temperature. Brush with oil before and during roasting–the oil will seal in the juices.

- For a juicier hamburger add cold water to the beef before grilling (1/2 cup to 1 pound of meat).

- To freeze meatballs, place them on a cookie sheet until frozen. Place in plastic bags and they will stay separated so that you may remove as many as you want.

- To keep cauliflower white while cooking–add a little milk to the water.

- When boiling corn, add sugar to the water instead of salt. Salt will toughen the corn.

- To ripen tomatoes–put them in a brown paper bag in a dark pantry and they will ripen overnight.

- Do not use soda to keep vegetables green. It destroys Vitamin C.

- When cooking cabbage, place a small tin cup or can half full of vinegar on the stove near the cabbage. It will absorb all odor from it.

- Potatoes soaked in salt water for 20 minutes before baking will bake more rapidly.

- Let raw potatoes stand in cold water for at least half an hour before frying to improve the crispness of French fried potatoes.

- Use greased muffin tins as molds when baking stuffed green peppers.

- A few drops of lemon juice in the water will whiten boiled potatoes.

- Buy mushrooms before they "open." When stems and caps are attached snugly, mushrooms are truly fresh.

- Do not use metal bowls when mixing salads. Use wooden, glass or china.

- Lettuce keeps better if you store in refrigerator without washing first so that the leaves are dry. Wash the day you are going to use.

- To keep celery crisp–stand it up in a pitcher of cold, salted water and refrigerate.

- Don't despair if you've oversalted the gravy. Stir in some instant mashed potatoes and you'll repair the damage. Just add a little more liquid to offset the thickening.

CALORIE  COUNTER

Beverages

Apple juice, 6 oz.	90
Coffee (black/unsw.)	0
Cola type, 12 oz.	115
Cranberry juice, 6 oz.	115
Ginger ale, 12 oz.	115
Grape juice, (prepared from frozen concentrate), 6 oz.	142
Lemonade (prepared from frozen concentrate), 6 oz.	85
Milk	
protein fortified, 1 c.	105
skim, 1 c.	90
whole, 1 c.	160
Orange juice, 6 oz.	85
Pineapple juice, unsweetened, 6 oz.	95
Root beer, 12 oz.	150
Tonic (quinine water), 12 oz.	132

Breads

Corn Bread, 1 small square	130
Dumplings, 1 med.	70
French Toast, 1 slice	135
Muffins	
bran, 1 muffin	106
blueberry, 1 muffin	110
corn, 1 muffin	125
English, 1 muffin	280
Melba Toast, 1 slice	25
Pancakes, 1-4 in.	60
Pumpernickel, 1 slice	75
Rye, 1 slice	60
Waffles, 1	216
White, 1 slice	60-70
Whole wheat, 1 slice	55-65

Cereals

Corn Flakes, 1 cup.	105
Cream of Wheat, 1 cup	120
Oatmeal, 1 cup	148
Rice Flakes, 1 cup	105
Shredded Wheat, 1 biscuit	100
Sugar Krisps, 3/4 cup	110

Crackers

Graham, 1 cracker	15-30
Rye Crisp, 1 cracker	35
Saltine, 1 cracker	17-20
Wheat Thins, 1 cracker	9

Dairy Products

Butter or Margarine, 1 T	100
Cheese	
American Cheese, 1 oz.	100
Camembert, 1 oz.	85
Cheddar, 1 oz.	115
Cottage Cheese, 1 oz.	30
Mozzarella, 1 oz.	90
Parmesan, 1 oz.	130
Ricotta, 1 oz.	50
Roquefort, 1 oz.	105
Swiss, 1 oz.	105
Cream	
Light, 1 T	30
Heavy, 1 T.	55
Sour, 1 T	45
Hot chocolate, with milk, 1 c.	277
Milk chocolate, 1 oz.	145-155
Yogurt	
made w/ whole milk, 1 c.	150-165
made w/ skimmed milk, 1 c.	125

Eggs

Fried, 1 large	100
Poached or boiled, 1 large	75-80
Scrambled or in omelet, 1 large	110-130

Fish and Seafood

Bass, 4 oz.	105
Salmon, broiled or baked, 3 oz.	155
Sardines canned in oil, 3 oz.	170
Trout, fried, 3 1/2 oz.	220
Tuna, in oil, 3 oz.	170
Tuna, in water, 3 oz.	110

Calorie Counter, Continued

Fruits

Apple, 1 medium 80-100
Applesauce, sweetened, 1/2 c. 90-115
Applesauce, unsweetened,
  1/2 c. 50
Banana, 1 medium 85
Blueberries, 1/2 c. 45
Cantaloupe melon, 1/2 c. 24
Cherries (pitted), raw, 1/2 c. 40
Grapefruit, 1/2 medium 55
Grapes, 1/2 c. ....35 - 55
Honeydew melon, 1/2 c. 55
Mango, 1 medium 90
Orange, 1 medium 65-75
Peach, 1 medium 35
Pear, 1 medium 60-100
Pineapple, fresh, 1/2 c. 40
Pineapple, canned in syrup, 1/2 c. 95
Plum, 1 medium 30
Strawberries, fresh, 1/2 c. 30
Strawberries, frozen
  and sweetened, 1/2 c. 120-140
Tangerine, 1 large 39
Watermelon, 1/2 c. 42

Meat and Poultry

Beef, ground (lean), 3 oz. 185
Beef, roast, 3 oz. 185
Chicken, broiled, 3 oz. 115
Lamb chop (lean), 3 oz. 175-200
Sirloin steak, 3 oz. 175
Tenderloin steak, 3 oz. 174
Top round steak, 3 oz. 162
Turkey, dark meat, 3 oz. 175
Turkey, white meat, 3 oz. 150
Veal cutlet, 3 oz. 156
Veal, roast, 3 oz. 176

Nuts

Almonds, 2 T. 105
Cashews, 2 T. 100
Peanuts, 2 T. 105
Peanut butter, 1 T. 95
Pecans, 2 T. 95
Pistachios, 2 T. 92
Walnuts, 2 T. 80

Pasta

Macaroni or spaghetti,
  3/4 c. cooked 115

Salad Dressings

Blue cheese, 1 T. 70
French, 1 T. 65
Italian, 1 T. 80
Mayonnaise, 1 T. 100
Olive oil, 1 T. 124
Russian, 1 T. 70
Salad oil, 1 T. 120

Soups

Bean, 1 c. 130-180
Beef noodle, 1 c. 70
Bouillon and consomme, 1 c. 30
Chicken noodle, 1 c. 65
Chicken with rice, 1 c. 50
Minestrone, 1 c. 80-150
Split pea, 1 c. 145-170
Tomato with milk, 1 c. 170
Vegetable, 1 c. 80-100

Vegetables

Asparagus, 1 c. 35
Broccoli, cooked, 1/2 c. 25
Cabbage, cooked, 1/2 c. 15-20
Carrots, cooked, 1/2 c. 25-30
Cauliflower, 1/2 c. 10-15
Corn (kernels), 1/2 c. 70
Green Beans, 1 c. 30
Lettuce, shredded, 1/2 c. 5
Mushrooms, canned, 1/2 c. 20
Onions, cooked, 1/2 c. 30
Peas, green, cooked, 1/2 c. 60
Potato
  baked, 1 medium 90
  chips, 8-10 100
  mashed, with milk
  and butter, 1 c. 200-300
Spinach, 1 cup 40
Tomato
  raw, 1 medium 25
  cooked, 1/2 c. 30

MEASUREMENTS & SUBSTITUTIONS

Measurements

a pinch	1/8 teaspoon or less
3 teaspoons	1 tablespoon
4 tablespoons	1/4 cup
8 tablespoons	1/2 cup
12 tablespoons	3/4 cup
16 tablespoons	1 cup
2 cups	1 pint
4 cups	1 quart
4 quarts	1 gallon
8 quarts	1 peck
4 pecks	1 bushel
16 ounces	1 pound
32 ounces	1 quart
8 ounces liquid	1 cup
1 ounce liquid	2 tablespoons

(For liquid and dry measurements use standard measuring spoons and cups. All measurements are level.)

Substitutions

Ingredient	Quantity	Substitute
self rising flour	1 cup	1 cup all-purpose flour, 1/2 tsp. salt, and 1 tsp. baking powder
cornstarch	1 tablespoon	2 T. flour or 2 tsp. quick-cooking tapioca
baking powder	1 teaspoon	1/4 tsp. baking soda plus 1/2 tsp. cream of tartar
powdered sugar	1 cup	1 c. granulated sugar plus 1 tsp. cornstarch
brown sugar	1/2 cup	2 T. molasses in 1/2 c. granulated sugar
sour milk	1 cup	1 T. lemon juice or vinegar plus sweet milk to make 1 c. (let stand 5 minutes).
whole milk	1 cup	1/2 c. evaporated milk plus 1/2 c. water
cracker crumbs	3/4 cup	1 c. bread crumbs
chocolate	1 square (1 oz.)	3 or 4 T. cocoa plus 1 T. butter*
fresh herbs	1 tablespoon	1 tsp. dried herbs
fresh onion	1 small	1 T. instant minced onion, rehydrated
dry mustard	1 teaspoon	1 T. prepared mustard
tomato juice	1 cup	1/2 c. tomato sauce plus 1/2 c. water
catsup or chili sauce	1 cup	1 c. tomato sauce plus 1/2 c. sugar and 2 T. vinegar (for use in cooking).
dates	1 lb.	1 1/2 c. dates, pitted and cut
bananas	3 medium	1 c. mashed
min. marshmallows	10	1 lg. marshmallow

*In substituting cocoa for chocolate in cakes, the amount of flour must be reduced.
Brown and White Sugars: Usually may be used interchangeably.

MICROWAVE HINTS

1. Place an open box of hardened brown sugar in the microwave oven with 1 cup hot water. Microwave at high for 1 1/2 to 2 minutes for 1/2 pound or 2 to 3 minutes for 1 pound.
2. Soften hard ice cream by microwaving at 30% power. One pint will take 15 to 30 seconds; one quart, 30-45 seconds; and one-half gallon 45-60 seconds.
3. One stick of butter or margarine will soften in 1 minute when microwaved at 20% power.
4. Soften one 8-ounce package of cream cheese by microwaving at 30% power for 2 to 2 1/2 minutes. One 3-ounce package of cream cheese will soften in 1 1/2 to 2 minutes.
5. Thaw frozen orange juice right in the container. Remove the top metal lid. Place the opened container in the microwave and heat on high power 30 seconds for 6 ounces and 45 seconds for 12 ounces.
6. Thaw whipped topping…a 4 1/2 ounce carton will thaw in 1 minute on the defrost setting. Whipped topping should be slightly firm in the center but it will blend well when stirred. Do not overthaw!
7. Soften Jello that has set up too hard–perhaps you were to chill it until slightly thickened and forgot it. Heat on a low power setting for a very short time.
8. Heat hot packs in a microwave oven. A wet finger tip towel will take about 25 seconds. It depends on the temperature of the water used to wet the towel.
9. To scald milk, cook 1 cup for 2 to 2 1/2 minutes, stirring once each minute.
10. To make dry bread crumbs, cut 6 slices bread into 1/2-inch cubes. Microwave in 3-quart casserole 6-7 minutes, or until dry, stirring after 3 minutes. Crush in blender.
11. Refresh stale potato chips, crackers or other snacks of such type by putting a plateful in the microwave oven for about 30-45 seconds. Let stand for 1 minute to crisp. Cereals can also be crisped.
12. Nuts will be easier to shell if you place 2 cups of nuts in a 1-quart casserole with 1 cup of water. Cook for 4 to 5 minutes and the nutmeats will slip out whole after cracking the shell.
13. For stamp collectors: place a few drops of water on stamp to be removed from envelope. Heat in the microwave for 20 seconds and the stamp will come right off.
14. Using a round dish instead of a square one eliminates overcooked corners in baking cakes.
15. A crusty coating of chopped walnuts surrounding many microwave cooked cakes and quick breads enhances the looks and eating quality. Sprinkle a layer of medium, finely chopped walnuts evenly onto the bottom and side of a ring pan or bundt cake pan. Pour in batter and microwave as recipe directs.
16. Do not salt foods on the surface as it causes dehydration and toughens the food. Salt after you remove from the oven unless the recipe calls for using salt in the mixture.
17. Heat left-over custard and use it as frosting for a cake.
18. Melt marshmallow cream in the microwave oven. Half of a 7-ounce jar will melt in 35-40 seconds on high. Stir to blend.
19. Toast coconut in the microwave. Watch closely as it browns quickly once it begins to brown. Spread 1/2 cup coconut in a pie plate and cook for 3-4 minutes, stirring every 30 seconds after 2 minutes.

Herbs & Spices

Get acquainted with herbs and spices. Add in small amounts, 1/4 teaspoon for each 4 servings. Taste before adding more. Crush dried herbs or snip fresh herbs before using. If substituting fresh for dried, use 3 times more fresh herbs.

Basil
Sweet warm flavor with an aromatic odor, used whole or ground. Good with lamb, fish, roast, stews, ground beef, vegetables, dressing and omelets.

Bay Leaves
A pungent flavor, use whole leaf but remove before serving. Good in vegetable dishes, fish and seafood, stews and pickles.

Caraway
Has a spicy smell and aromatic taste. Use in cakes, breads, soups, cheese and sauerkraut.

Chives
Sweet mild flavor of onion, this herb is excellent in salads, fish, soups and potatoes.

Curry Powder
A number of spices combined to proper proportions to give a distinct flavor to such dishes as meat, poultry, fish and vegetables.

Dill
Both seeds and leaves of dill are flavorful. Leaves may be used to garnish or cook with fish, soup, dressings, potatoes and beans. Leaves or the whole plant may be used to spice dill pickles.

Fennel
Both seeds and leaves are used. It has a sweet hot flavor. Use in small quantities in pies and baked goods. Leaves can be boiled with fish.

Ginger
A pungent root, this aromatic spice is sold fresh, dried, or ground. Used in pickles, preserves, cakes, cookies, soups and meat dishes.

Herbs & Spices

Marjoram   May be used both dry or green. Used to flavor fish, poultry, omelets, lamb, stew, stuffing and tomato juice.

Mint   Leaves are aromatic with a cool flavor. Excellent in beverages, fish, cheese, lamb, soup, peas, carrots, and fruit desserts.

Oregano   Strong aromatic odor, use whole or ground to spice tomato juice, fish, eggs, pizza, omelets, chili, stew, gravy, poultry and vegetables.

Paprika   A bright red pepper, this spice is used in meat, vegetables and soups. Can be used as a garnish for potatoes, salads or eggs.

Parsley   Best when used fresh but can be used dry. Use as garnish or seasoning. Try in fish, omelets, soup, meat, stuffing and mixed greens.

Rosemary   Very aromatic, used fresh or dried. Season fish, stuffing, beef, lamb, poultry, onions, eggs and bread.

Saffron   Orange yellow in color, this spice is used to flavor or color foods. Use in soup, chicken, rice and fancy breads.

Sage   Use fresh or dried. The flowers are sometimes used in salads. May be used in tomato juice, fish, fondue, omelets, beef, poultry, stuffing, cheese spreads, cornbread and biscuits.

Tarragon   Leaves have a pungent, hot taste. Use to flavor sauces, salads, meat, poultry, tomatoes and dressings.

NAPKIN FOLDING

General Tips:
Use linen napkins if possible, well starched.
For the more complicated folds, 24 inch napkins work best.
Practice the folds with newspapers.
Children can help. Once they learn the folds, they will have fun!

Shield

This fold is easy. Elegant with Monogram in Corner.

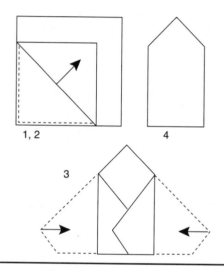

Instructions:
1. Fold into quarter size. If monogrammed, ornate corner should face down.
2. Turn up folded corner three-quarters.
3. Overlap right and left side points.
4. Turn over; adjust sides so that they are even, single point in center.
5. Place point up or down on plate, or left of plate.

Rosette

Elegant on Plate.

Instructions:
1. Fold top and bottom edges to the center, leaving 1/2" opening along the center.
2. Pleat firmly from the left edge. Sharpen edges with hot iron.
3. Pinch center together. If necessary, use small piece of pipe cleaner to secure and top with single flower.
4. Spread out rosette.

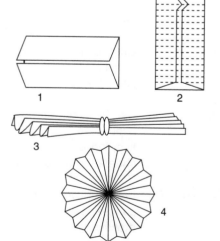

NAPKIN FOLDING

Fan

Pretty in Napkin Ring, or Top of Plate.

Instructions:
1. Fold top and bottom edges to the center.
2. Fold top and bottom edges to center a second time.
3. Pleat firmly from the left edge. Sharpen edges with a hot iron.
4. Spread out fan. Balance flat folds on each side on table. Well-starched napkins will hold the shape.

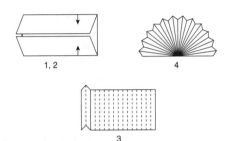

Candle

Easy to do; can be decorated.

Instructions:
1. Fold into triangle, point at top.
2. Turn lower edge up 1".
3. Turn over, folded edge down.
4. Roll tightly from left to right.
5. Tuck in corner. Stand upright.

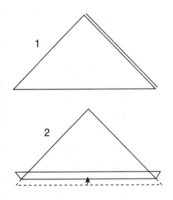

Lily

Effective and Pretty on Table.

Instructions:
1. Fold napkin into quarters.
2. Fold into triangle, closed corner to open points.
3. Turn two points over to other side. (Two points are on either side of closed point.) Pleat.
4. Place closed end in glass. Pull down two points on each side and shape.

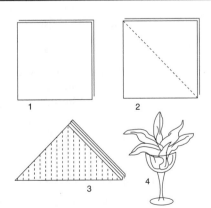

VEGETABLE TIME TABLE

Vegetable	Cooking Method	Time
Asparagus Tips	Boiled..................	10-15 minutes
Artichokes, French	Boiled..................	40 minutes
	Steamed...............	45-60 minutes
Beans, Lima	Boiled..................	20-40 minutes
	Steamed...............	60 minutes
Beans, String	Boiled..................	15-35 minutes
	Steamed...............	60 minutes
Beets, young with skin	Boiled..................	30 minutes
	Steamed...............	60 minutes
	Baked..................	70-90 minutes
Beets, old	Boiled or Steamed...	1-2 hours
Broccoli, flowerets	Boiled..................	5-10 minutes
Broccoli, stems	Boiled..................	20-30 minutes
Brussel Sprouts	Boiled..................	20-30 minutes
Cabbage, chopped	Boiled..................	10-20 minutes
	Steamed...............	25 minutes
Cauliflower, stem down	Boiled..................	20-30 minutes
Cauliflower, flowerets	Boiled..................	8-10 minutes
Carrots, cut across	Boiled..................	8-10 minutes
	Steamed...............	40 minutes
Corn, green, tender	Boiled..................	5-10 minutes
	Steamed...............	15 minutes
	Baked..................	20 minutes
Corn on the cob	Boiled..................	8-10 minutes
	Steamed...............	15 minutes
Eggplant, whole	Boiled..................	30 minutes
	Steamed...............	40 minutes
	Baked..................	45 minutes
Parsnips	Boiled..................	25-40 minutes
	Steamed...............	60 minutes
	Baked..................	60-75 minutes
Peas, green	Boiled or Steamed...	5-15 minutes
Potatoes	Boiled..................	20-40 minutes
	Steamed...............	60 minutes
	Baked..................	45-60 minutes
Pumpkin or Squash	Boiled..................	20-40 minutes
	Steamed...............	45 minutes
	Baked..................	60 minutes
Tomatoes	Boiled..................	5-15 minutes
Turnips	Boiled..................	25-40 minutes

BUYING GUIDE
Fresh Vegetables and Fruits

Experience is the best teacher in choosing quality, but here are a few pointers on buying some of the fruits and vegetables.

Asparagus: Stalks should be tender and firm, tips should be close and compact. Choose the stalks with very little white–they are more tender. Use asparagus soon–it toughens rapidly.

Beans, Snap: Those with small seeds inside the pods are best. Avoid beans with dry-looking pods.

Berries: Select plump, solid berries with good color. Avoid stained containers, indicating wet or leaky berries. Berries such as blackberries and raspberries with clinging caps may be under-ripe. Strawberries without caps may be too ripe.

Broccoli, Brussel Sprouts, and Cauliflower: Flower clusters on broccoli and cauliflower should be tight and close together. Brussel sprouts should be firm and compact. Smudgy, dirty spots may indicate insects.

Cabbage and Head Lettuce: Choose heads heavy for size. Avoid cabbage with worm holes, lettuce with discoloration or soft rot.

Cucumbers: Choose long, slender cucumbers for best quality. May be dark or medium green but yellowed ones are undesirable.

Melons: In cantaloupes, thick close netting on the rind indicates best quality. Cantaloupes are ripe when the stem scar is smooth and space between the netting is yellow or yellow-green. They are best when fully ripe with fruity odor.

Honeydews are ripe when rind has creamy to yellowish color and velvety texture. Immature honeydews are whitish-green.

Ripe watermelons have some yellow color on one side. If melons are white or pale green on one side, they are not ripe.

Oranges, Grapefruit, and Lemons: Choose those heavy for their size. Smoother, thinner skins usually indicate more juice. Most skin markings do not affect quality. Oranges with a slight greenish tinge may be just as ripe as fully colored ones. Light or greenish-yellow lemons are more tart than deep yellow ones. Avoid citrus fruits showing withered, sunken, or soft areas.

Peas and Lima Beans: Select pods that are well-filled but not bulging. Avoid dried, spotted, yellowed, or flabby pods.

TABLE FOR DRIED FRUITS

Fruit	Cooking Time	Amount of Sugar or Honey
Apricots	About 40 minutes	1/4 c. for each cup of fruit
Figs	About 30 minutes	1 T. for each cup of fruit
Peaches	About 45 minutes	1/4 c. for each cup of fruit
Prunes	About 45 minutes	2 T. for each cup of fruit

BAKING PERFECT BREADS

Proportions

Biscuits ....To 1 c. flour use 1 1/4 tsp. Baking Powder
Muffins ....To 1 c. flour use 1 1/2 tsp. Baking Powder
Popovers...To 1 c. flour use 1 1/4 tsp. Baking Powder
Waffles ....To 1 c. flour use 1 1/4 tsp. Baking Powder
Cake with oil...To 1 c. flour use 1 tsp. Baking Powder

Rules for Use of Leavening Agents

1. To 1 teaspoon soda use 2 1/4 teaspoons cream of tartar, or 2 cups freshly soured milk, or 1 cup molasses.
2. In simple flour mixtures, use 2 teaspoons baking powder to leaven 1 cup flour. Reduce this amount 1/2 teaspoon for each egg used.
3. To substitute soda and an acid for baking powder, divide the amount of baking powder by 4. Take that as your measure of and add the acid according to rule 1 above.

Proportions for Batters and Dough

Pour Batter ....To 1 cup liquid use 1 cup flour
Drop Batter.............................To 1 cup liquid use 2 to 2 1/2 cups flour
Soft Dough ....To 1 cup liquid use 3 to 3 1/2 cups flour
Stiff Dough ....To 1 cup liquid use 4 cups flour

Hints for Baking Breads

Kneading the dough for a half minute after mixing improves the texture of baking powder biscuits.

Use cooking or salad oil in waffles and hot cakes in the place of shortening. No extra pan or bowl to melt the shortening and no waiting.

When bread is baking, a small dish of water in the oven will help to keep the crust from getting hard.

Dip the spoon in hot water to measure shortening, butter, etc., the fat will slip out more easily.

Small amounts of leftover corn may be added to pancake batter for variety.

To make bread crumbs, use fine cutter of the food grinder and tie a large paper bag over the spout to prevent flying crumbs.

When you are doing any sort of baking, you get better results if you remember to pre-heat your cookie sheet, muffin tins, or cake pans.

Oven Temperature Chart

Breads	Minutes	Temperature
Loaf	45 - 60	350° - 400°
Rolls	15 - 30	350° - 425°
Biscuits	10 - 15	400° - 450°
Muffins	15 - 25	400° - 425°
Cornbread	20 - 25	400° - 425°
Nut Bread	60 - 75	350°
Gingerbread	35 - 50	350° - 375°

BAKING PERFECT DESSERTS

For Perfect Cookies

Cookie dough that is to be rolled is much easier to handle after it has been refrigerated for 10 to 30 minutes. This keeps the dough from sticking, even though it may be soft. If not done, the soft dough may require more flour and too much flour makes cookies hard and brittle. In rolling, take out on a floured board, only as much dough as can be easily managed. Flour the rolling pin slightly and roll lightly to desired thickness. Cut shapes close together and keep all trimmings for the last roll. Place pans or sheets in upper third of oven. Watch cookies carefully while baking to avoid burning edges. When sprinkling sugar on cookies, try putting it into a salt shaker. It saves time.

For Perfect Pies and Cakes

- A pie crust will be more easily made and better if all the ingredients are cool.

- The lower crust should be placed in the pan so that it covers the surface smoothly. Be sure no air lurks beneath the surface, for it will push the crust out of shape in baking.

- Folding the top crust over the lower crust before crimping will keep the juices in the pie.

- In making custard type pies, bake at a high temperature for about ten minutes to prevent a soggy crust. Then finish baking at a low temperature.

- Fill cake pans about 2/3 full and spread batter well into corners and to the sides, leaving a slight hollow in the center.

- The cake is done when it shrinks from the sides of the pan or if it springs back when touched lightly with the finger.

- After a cake comes from the oven, it should be placed on a rack for about five minutes. Then the sides should be loosened and the cake turned out on a rack to finish cooling.

- Cakes should not be frosted until thoroughly cool.

- To prevent crust from becoming soggy with cream pie, sprinkle crust with powdered sugar.

Temperature Chart

Food	Temperature	Time
Butter Cake, loaf	300° - 350°	50 - 80 min.
Butter Cake, layer	350° - 375°	25 - 35 min.
Cake, angel	350° - 375°	35 - 50 min.
Cake, sponge	350° - 375°	12 - 40 min.
Cake, fruit	250° - 275°	3 - 4 hours
Cookies, rolled	375° - 400°	6 - 12 min.
Cookies, drop	350° - 400°	8 - 15 min.
Cream Puffs	300° - 350°	45 - 60 min.
Meringue	300° - 350°	12 - 15 min.
Pie Crust (shell)	400° - 450°	10 - 12 min.

Food Quantities for Serving 25, 50, and 100 People

Food	25 Servings	50 Servings	100 Servings
Sandwiches:			
Bread	50 slices or 3 (1-lb.) loaves	100 slices or 6 (1-lb.) loaves	200 slices or 12 (1-lb.) loaves
Butter	1/2 pound	3/4 to 1 pound	1 1/2 pounds
Mayonnaise	1 cup	2 to 3 cups	4 to 6 cups
Mixed Filling (meat, eggs, fish)	1 1/2 quarts	2 1/2 to 3 quarts	5 to 6 quarts
Mixed Filling (sweet-fruit)	1 quart	1 3/4 to 2 quarts	2 1/2 to 4 quarts
Lettuce	1 1/2 heads	2 1/2 to 3 heads	5 to 6 heads
Meat, Poultry, or Fish:			
Hot dogs (beef)	6 1/2 pounds	13 pounds	25 pounds
Hamburger	9 pounds	18 pounds	35 pounds
Turkey or Chicken	13 pounds	25 to 35 pounds	50 to 75 pounds
Fish, large whole (round)	13 pounds	25 pounds	50 pounds
Fish fillets or steak	7 1/2 pounds	15 pounds	30 pounds
Salads, Casseroles:			
Potato Salad	4 1/4 quarts	1 1/4 gallons	4 1/4 gallons
Scalloped Potatoes	4 1/2 quarts or 1 12" x 20" pan	8 1/2 quarts	17 quarts
Spaghetti	1 1/4 gallons	2 1/2 gallons	5 gallons
Baked Beans	3/4 gallon	1 1/4 gallons	2 1/2 gallons
Jello Salad	3/4 gallon	1 1/4 gallons	2 1/2 gallons
Ice Cream:			
Brick	3 1/4 quarts	6 1/2 quarts	12 1/2 quarts
Bulk	2 1/4 quarts	4 1/2 quarts or 1 1/4 gallons	9 quarts or 2 1/2 gallons
Beverages:			
Coffee	1/2 pound and 1 1/2 gal. water	1 pound and 3 gal. water	2 pounds and 6 gal. water
Tea	1/12 pound and 1 1/2 gal. water	1/6 pound 3 gal. water	1/3 pound and 6 gal. water
Lemonade	10 to 15 lemons, 1 1/2 gal. water	20 to 30 lemons, 3 gal. water	40 to 60 lemons, 6 gal. water
Desserts:			
Watermelon	37 1/2 pounds	75 pounds	150 pounds
Cake	1 10" x 12" sheet cake 2 8" layer cakes	1 12" x 20" sheet cakes 3 10" layer cakes	2 12" x 20" sheet cakes 6 10" layer cakes
Whipping Cream	1 pint	1 quart	2 quarts

EQUIVALENCY CHART

FOOD	QUANTITY	YIELD
unsifted flour	3 3/4 cups	1 pound
sifted flour	4 cups	1 pound
sifted cake flour	4 1/2 cups	1 pound
rye flour	5 cups	1 pound
flour	1 pound	4 cups
baking powder	5 1/2 ounces	1 cup
cornmeal	3 cups	1 pound
cornstarch	3 cups	1 pound
lemon	1 medium	3 tablespoons juice
apple	1 medium	1 cup
orange	3-4 medium	1 cup juice
onion	1 medium	1/2 cup
unshelled walnuts	1 pound	1 1/2 to 1 3/4 cups
sugar	2 cups	1 pound
powdered sugar	3 1/2 cups	1 pound
brown sugar	2 1/2 cups	1 pound
spaghetti	7 ounces	4 cups cooked
noodles (uncooked)	4 ounces (1 1/2 - 2 cups)	2-3 cups cooked
macaroni (uncooked)	4 ounces (1 1/4 cups)	2 1/4 cups cooked
macaroni (cooked)	6 cups	8-ounce package
noodles (cooked)	7 cups	8-ounce package
long-grain rice (uncooked)	1 cup	3-4 cups cooked
saltine crackers	28 crackers	1 cup fine crumbs
butter	1 stick or 1/4 lb.	1/2 cup
cocoa	4 cups	1 pound
chocolate (bitter)	1 ounce	1 square
coconut	2 2/3 cups	1 1/2 pound carton
marshmallows	16	1/4 pound
graham crackers	14 squares	1 cup fine crumbs
vanilla wafers	22	1 cup fine crumbs
bread	1 1/2 slices	1 cup soft crumbs
bread	1 slice	1/4 cup fine, dry crumbs
egg whites	8-10	1 cup
egg yolks	10-12	1 cup
egg	4-5 whole	1 cup
flavored gelatin	3 1/4 ounces	1/2 cup
unflavored gelatin	1/4 ounce	1 tablespoon
nuts (chopped)	1 cup	1/4 pound
almonds	3 1/2 cups	1 pound
walnuts (broken)	3 cups	1 pound
raisins	1 pound	3 1/2 cups
rice	2 1/3 cups	1 pound
American cheese (grated)	5 cups	1 pound
American cheese (cubed)	2 2/3 cups	1 pound
cream cheese	6 2/3 tablespoons	3-ounce package
zwieback (crumbled)	4	1 cup
banana (mashed)	1 medium	1/3 cup
coffee (ground)	5 cups	1 pound
evaporated milk	1 cup	3 cups whipped

TERMS USED IN COOKING

Au gratin: Topped with crumbs and/or cheese and browned in the oven or under the broiler.

Au jus: Served in its own juices.

Baste: To moisten foods during cooking with pan drippings or special sauce to add flavor and prevent drying.

Bisque: A thick cream soup.

Blanch: To immerse in rapidly boiling water and allow to cook slightly.

Cream: To soften a fat, especially butter, by beating it at room temperature. Butter and sugar are often creamed together, making a smooth, soft paste.

Crimp: To seal the edges of a two-crust pie either by pinching them at intervals with the fingers or by pressing them together with the tines of a fork.

Crudites: An assortment of raw vegetables, i.e. carrots, broccoli, mushrooms, served as an hors d'oeuvre often accompanied by a dip.

Degrease: To remove fat from the surface of stews, soups, or stock. Usually cooled in the refrigerator, so that fat hardens and is easily removed.

Dredge: To coat lightly with flour, cornmeal, etc.

Entree: The main course.

Fold: To incorporate a delicate substance, such as whipped cream or beaten egg whites, into another substance without releasing air bubbles. A spatula is used to gently bring part of the mixture from the bottom of the bowl to the top. The process is repeated, while slowly rotating the bowl, until the ingredients are thoroughly blended.

Glaze: To cover with a glossy coating, such as a melted and somewhat diluted jelly for fruit desserts.

Julienne: To cut vegetables, fruits, or cheeses into match-shaped slivers.

Marinade: To allow food to stand in a liquid to tenderize or to add flavor.

Meuniere: Dredged with flour and sauteed in butter.

Mince: To chop or cut food into very small pieces.

Parboil: To boil until partially cooked; to blanch. Usually this procedure is followed by final cooking in a seasoned sauce.

Pare: To remove the outermost skin of a fruit or vegetable.

Poach: To cook very gently in hot liquid kept just below the boiling point.

Puree: To mash foods until perfectly smooth by hand, by rubbing through a sieve or food mill, or by whirling in a blender or food processor.

Refresh: To run cold water over food that has been parboiled, to stop the cooking process quickly.

Saute: To cook and/or brown food in a small quantity of hot oil.

Scald: To heat to just below the boiling point, when tiny bubbles appear at the edge of the saucepan.

Simmer: To cook in liquid just below the boiling point. The surface of the liquid should be barely moving, broken from time to time by slowly rising bubbles.

Steep: To let food stand in (hot) liquid to extract or to enhance flavor, like tea in hot water or poached fruits in sugar syrup.

Toss: To combine ingredients with a lifting motion.

Whip: To beat rapidly to incorporate air and produce expansion, as in heavy cream or egg whites.

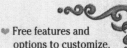

Create your own cookbook
with Cookbooks by Morris Press

Call for Free Information (no obligation)

1-800-445-6621 ext. CB

Or complete and send the Business Reply Card
below. See other side for details.